920 THE

They died too young

THEY★DIED
TOO YOUNG

B MARLEY • FREDDIE MERCURY • MARILYN MONROE • JIM MORRISON • RIVER PHOENIX • ELVIS
RPENTER • KURT COBAIN • JAMES DEAN • ISADORA DUNCAN • MARVIN GAYE • JIMI HENDRIX • E
ARILYN MONROE • JIM MORRISON • RIVER PHOENIX • ELVIS PRESLEY • AYRTON SENNA • RUDOLPH V.
SADORA DUNCAN • MARVIN GAYE • JIMI HENDRIX • BUDDY HOLLY • MARTIN LUTHER KING • BRUC
OENIX • ELVIS PRESLEY • AYRTON SENNA • RUDOLPH VALENTINO • SID VICIOUS • MARC BOLAN • B
NDRIX • BUDDY HOLLY • MARTIN LUTHER KING • BRUCE LEE • JOHN LENNON • BOB MARLEY • FRE
DOLPH VALENTINO • SID VICIOUS • MARC BOLAN • BUSBY BABES • KAREN CARPENTER • KURT CO
NG • BRUCE LEE • JOHN LENNON • BOB MARLEY • FREDDIE MERCURY • MARILYN MONROE • JIM M
OLAN • BUSBY BABES • KAREN CARPENTER • KURT COBAIN • JAMES DEAN • ISADORA DUNCAN • I
ARLEY • FREDDIE MERCURY • MARILYN MONROE • JIM MORRISON • RIVER PHOENIX • ELVIS PRESLEY
KURT COBAIN • JAMES DEAN • ISADORA DUNCAN • MARVIN GAYE • JIMI HENDRIX • BUDDY HOLLY • I
IM MORRISON • RIVER PHOENIX • ELVIS PRESLEY • AYRTON SENNA • RUDOLPH VALENTINO • SID VIC
MARVIN GAYE • JIMI HENDRIX • BUDDY HOLLY • MARTIN LUTHER KING • BRUCE LEE • JOHN LENNON
AYRTON SENNA • RUDOLPH VALENTINO • SID VICIOUS • MARC BOLAN • BUSBY BABES • KAREN CAR
MARTIN LUTHER KING • BRUCE LEE • JOHN LENNON • BOB MARLEY • FREDDIE MERCURY • MARILY
D VICIOUS • MARC BOLAN • BUSBY BABES • KAREN CARPENTER • KURT COBAIN • JAMES DEAN • ISA
NNON • BOB MARLEY • FREDDIE MERCURY • MARILYN MONROE • JIM MORRISON • RIVER PHOENIX
AREN CARPENTER • KURT COBAIN • JAMES DEAN • ISADORA DUNCAN • MARVIN GAYE • JIMI HENDRI
MARILYN MONROE • JIM MORRISON • RIVER PHOENIX • ELVIS PRESLEY • AYRTON SENNA • RUDOLF
EAN • ISADORA DUNCAN • MARVIN GAYE • JIMI HENDRIX • BUDDY HOLLY • MARTIN LUTHER KING • B
HOENIX • ELVIS PRESLEY • AYRTON SENNA • RUDOLPH VALENTINO • SID VICIOUS • MARC BOLAN • B
ENDRIX • BUDDY HOLLY • MARTIN LUTHER KING • BRUCE LEE • JOHN LENNON • BOB MARLEY • FRE
DOLPH VALENTINO • SID VICIOUS • MARC BOLAN • BUSBY BABES • KAREN CARPENTER • KURT CO
NG • BRUCE LEE • JOHN LENNON • BOB MARLEY • FREDDIE MERCURY • MARILYN MONROE • JIM M
OLAN • BUSBY BABES • KAREN CARPENTER • KURT COBAIN • JAMES DEAN • ISADORA DUNCAN • I
ARLEY • FREDDIE MERCURY • MARILYN MONROE • JIM MORRISON • RIVER PHOENIX • ELVIS PRESLEY
KURT COBAIN • JAMES DEAN • ISADORA DUNCAN • MARVIN GAYE • JIMI HENDRIX • BUDDY HOLLY • I
IM MORRISON • RIVER PHOENIX • ELVIS PRESLEY • AYRTON SENNA • RUDOLPH VALENTINO • SID VIC
MARVIN GAYE • JIMI HENDRIX • BUDDY HOLLY • MARTIN LUTHER KING • BRUCE LEE • JOHN LENNON
AYRTON SENNA • RUDOLPH VALENTINO • SID VICIOUS • MARC BOLAN • BUSBY BABES • KAREN CAR
MARTIN LUTHER KING • BRUCE LEE • JOHN LENNON • BOB MARLEY • FREDDIE MERCURY • MARILY
D VICIOUS • MARC BOLAN • BUSBY BABES • KAREN CARPENTER • KURT COBAIN • JAMES DEAN • ISA
NNON • BOB MARLEY • FREDDIE MERCURY • MARILYN MONROE • JIM MORRISON • RIVER PHOENIX
AREN CARPENTER • KURT COBAIN • JAMES DEAN • ISADORA DUNCAN • MARVIN GAYE • JIMI HENDRI
MARILYN MONROE • JIM MORRISON • RIVER PHOENIX • ELVIS PRESLEY • AYRTON SENNA • RUDOLF
EAN • ISADORA DUNCAN • MARVIN GAYE • JIMI HENDRIX • BUDDY HOLLY • MARTIN LUTHER KING • B
HOENIX • ELVIS PRESLEY • AYRTON SENNA • RUDOLPH VALENTINO • SID VICIOUS • MARC BOLAN • B
ENDRIX • BUDDY HOLLY • MARTIN LUTHER KING • BRUCE LEE • JOHN LENNON • BOB MARLEY • FRE
DOLPH VALENTINO • SID VICIOUS • MARC BOLAN • BUSBY BABES • KAREN CARPENTER • KURT CO
NG • BRUCE LEE • JOHN LENNON • BOB MARLEY • FREDDIE MERCURY • MARILYN MONROE • JIM M
OLAN • BUSBY BABES • KAREN CARPENTER • KURT COBAIN • JAMES DEAN • ISADORA DUNCAN • I
ARLEY • FREDDIE MERCURY • MARILYN MONROE • JIM MORRISON • RIVER PHOENIX • ELVIS PRESLEY

THEY DIED TOO YOUNG

THE BRIEF LIVES AND TRAGIC DEATHS OF
THE MEGA-STAR LEGENDS OF OUR TIME

EDITED BY TONY HALL

SMITHMARK

This edition published in 1996 by SMITHMARK Publishers,
a division of U.S. Media Holdings Inc.
16 East 32nd Street, New York, NY 10016.

SMITHMARK books are available for bulk purchase for sales promotion and premium use.
For details write or call the manager of special sales, SMITHMARK Publishers,
16 East 32nd Street, New York, NY 10016; (212) 532-6600.

Produced by Kingfisher Design, London
for
Parragon Publishing
13 Whiteladies Road
Clifton, Bristol BS8 1PB

ISBN: 0 765 19600X

Printed in Italy

10 9 8 7 6 5 4 3 2 1

ACKNOWLEDGEMENTS

Produced by Kingfisher Design, London

Design and Project Director: Pedro Prá-Lopez
Editor: Tony Hall

Typesetting and page formatting: Frank Landamore, Frances Prá-Lopez
Text Editors: Diana Craig, Linda Doeser
Index: Linda Doeser
Picture Research: Charlotte Deane

Colour Reprographics: Colour Quest Graphic Services, London

Material in this book has previously appeared in the
They Died Too Young Series, © Parragon Publishing 1995/6

Contents

PICTURE ACKNOWLEDGEMENTS

T = Top; B = Bottom; L = Left and R = Right

All images, including cover images, courtesy of
REX FEATURES
except for the following:

AQUARIUS
pages 26, 27, 28, 32BL, 43, 44, 51, 52, 53, 56TR, 57TR,
64TL, 68, 69TL, 71, 72TL, 75, 76TL, 77TL, 87, 88, 89

HULTON GETTY
pages 15, 16, 17, 47, 48, 49,

MANSELL COLLECTION
pages 30, 32TR, 33

TEXT ACKNOWLEDGEMENTS

This compilation has been abridged from the following titles, which first appeared in the
They Died Too Young Series, published by Parragon Publishing 1995/6:

Marc Bolan, Karen Carpenter, Marvin Gaye, Jimi Hendrix, Buddy Holly,
John Lennon and *Sid Vicious* by Tom Stockdale
The Busby Babes by David Sandison
Kurt Cobain by Andrew Gracie
James Dean, Martin Luther King and *Ayrton Senna* by A. Noble
Isadora Duncan and *Marilyn Monroe* by Esther Selsdon
Bob Marley by Millie Gilfoyle
Freddie Mercury by Simon Boyce
Bruce Lee and *Jim Morrison* by Jon E. Lewis
River Phoenix by Penny Stempel
Elvis Presley by Melissa Hardinge
Rudolph Valentino by Amy Dempsey

Kingfisher Design gratefully acknowledges the technical assistance of Peter Brady and Phil Le Monde of
Colour Quest Graphic Services Ltd, London in the preparation of this book

DEDICATED TO
THE MEMORY OF

Marc Bolan
1947-1977
Aged 29

Jimi Hendrix
1942-1970
Aged 27

Marilyn Monroe
1926-1962
Aged 36

Busby Babes
6 February
1958

Buddy Holly
1936-1959
Aged 22

Jim Morrison
1943-1971
Aged 27

Karen Carpenter
1950-1983
Aged 33

Martin Luther King
1929-1968
Aged 39

River Phoenix
1970-1993
Aged 23

Kurt Cobain
1967-1994
Aged 27

Bruce Lee
1940-1973
Aged 32

Elvis Presley
1935-1977
Aged 42

James Dean
1931-1955
Aged 24

John Lennon
1940-1980
Aged 40

Ayrton Senna
1960-1994
Aged 34

Isadora Duncan
1878-1927
Aged 49

Bob Marley
1945-1981
Aged 36

Rudolph Valentino
1895-1926
Aged 31

Marvin Gaye
1939-1984
Aged 44

Freddie Mercury
1946-1991
Aged 45

Sid Vicious
1957-1979
Aged 21

Introduction

No matter how much some of us might like to deny it, no one really wants to be an unknown, to be just 'someone else'. We all believe that we deserve better than what we have, and it is fame and celebrity – those modern touchstones – which seem able to solve all our problems, to open life's doors and give us the easy life we know is our due. To be famous, in one way or another, is everyone's dream.

But to make the magic work, fame has to be achieved against the odds. It is no good being born into wealth and fame: that does nothing for us. Instead, as in the lives of the men and women celebrated and mourned in this book, success must come, as if from nowhere, to those from ordinary backgrounds. Even more satisfying is if they come from grinding poverty and deprivation before achieving fame and fortune. It must have an air of romance and heroism about it, which of course makes the untimely deaths suffered by the stars here so much harder for us to bear. We are appalled by the utter waste, because these people had great talent. Many still exercise a profound influence. What might they have achieved if they had lived?

> **'Show me a hero and I will write you a tragedy.'**
>
> SCOTT FITZGERALD
> *American novelist*
> *of the 1920s Jazz Age*
> BORN: 1896 – DIED: 1940

Elvis, Marilyn Monroe, Kurt Cobain, John Lennon or Bob Marley became icons of their generations – even of the century – because of their natural-born gifts. If we can drag ourselves away from the grim fascination with their deaths, perhaps the most interesting aspect of these differing lives is the way in which a strange mix of upbringing, ego, commitment, influence, and fate managed to create unique gifts in seemingly ordinary people. In whichever sphere they worked, it was as if they had discovered something within themselves which spoke through modern mass communications, direct to us, and for us, and which propelled them to stardom. Whether they recognized it in themselves and were driven by ambition, fired by a vocation or were spotted by others and ruthlessly exploited, once that journey began the effect was the same. The image of the star, the role of leader, even the generating of social and cultural revolution engulfed them and for better or worse or, more usually, a mix of the two, they ceased to be the people they had once been.

A thread which links nearly everyone featured here – other than their early deaths – is a rootless, chameleon-like quality. In the course of their careers, names are changed, pasts are rewritten, marriages and partnerships come and go. It is as if fame speeds up their lives, bringing such unceasing public scrutiny that they lose track of who they are.

This is the turning point. In this created world which isolates them, in their own minds if nowhere else, they turn to 'crutches' to support their sense of reality. Whether alcohol, drugs, fast cars or a sublime belief that ill-health won't hurt them, a point is reached and crossed, and from there on it is only a matter of time.

Other figures in this book are tragic proof that fame, fortune and public acclaim are no defence against the lottery of fate – random accident or deadly disease. The terrible irony of pure chance – catching a different flight, for example – makes their early deaths even more poignant.

The lives and deaths of yet others in this book fall somewhere between the two extremes of self-destruction and sheer bad luck. Victims of their own charisma and star quality, they attracted both adulation and vicious hatred, ultimately dying at the hands of others.

All the people whose stories are told here achieved everything we would want for ourselves but in doing so somehow called down destruction. Sometimes the end was sudden, sometimes it came with a terrible inevitability, but always it came far too soon, leaving us to grieve and think of what might have been.

Tony Hall
London, 1 May, 1996

Marc Bolan

King of Glam Rock

1947–1977

Marc Bolan was born Mark Feld in London's Hackney Hospital on 30 September 1947, the second son of Sid and Phyllis Feld. His journey to musical fame began when Sid bought him Bill Haley and The Comets' 'See You Later Alligator', and his mother gave him an acoustic guitar for his ninth birthday.

The young Mark's overriding obsession was with clothes and by 1960 he was the leader of a local gang, posing at halls and clubs. He left school at the earliest opportunity, without qualifications or a job. He persuaded his mother to pay £100 for enrollment in a modelling school and also began to go to the television studios where the children's programme *The Five O'Clock Club* was recorded.

He struck up a friendship with one of the regular performers Allan Warren, and soon moved into a room in Warren's flat near Earls Court. He bought a harmonica and spent hours playing and talking up his talent. The two then had the idea of getting Mark on Warren's television show, and booked a session in a recording studio. Neither the songs from the session, nor the accompanying publicity shots, made any impression on the television company.

Mark wasn't going to let this stop him. He tried some new stage names and made friends with publicist Mike Pruskin, who agreed to become his manager. The change of name to Marc Bolan happened around the time, when the two were introduced to Decca's A&R man Dick Rowe. Rowe offered Bolan a recording deal and in September 1965 he went into the studio. The first release, 'The Wizard' and 'Beyond the Rising Sun', came to nothing. Decca brought out the second single in spring 1966 and when that too failed, Pruskin decided to quit.

Marc now needed another lucky break. A new direction was suggested when he met Simon Napier-Bell, a songwriter turned

Eccentric genius, hippy, Glam Rock star and 'Godfather of Punk'

manager, who sensed 'star quality'. He accepted Bolan's over-active imagination as part of an over-imaginative character.

Napier-Bell was managing The Yardbirds, but the idea of taking and breaking an artist from scratch appealed to him, especially a 'personality'. They chose 'Hippy Gumbo' as the single to launch the new-look Marc Bolan in November 1966, but the result was a flop.

Napier-Bell next tried linking Bolan with a noisy, band, called John's Children, that he had taken on in autumn 1966. Despite the single release of 'Desdemona' and a short tour of Germany supporting The Who, Marc left the band in under a year.

On 11 June 1967, *Melody Maker* carried an advertisement for musicians to join Bolan in a new band. The only successful candidate, drummer Peregrine Took, was an ideal partner. Bolan chose the new name, Tyrannosaurus Rex, and the band began recording. The sound was there from the start; with Bolan's slurred vocal delivery and Took's bongo beat. It was at this time that Bolan became friends with John Peel, then a DJ with Radio London, who decided to champion the band.

There was no room for Simon Napier-Bell on the hippy circuit and he dropped out. Producer Tony Visconti, however, was soon to see the band, and introduced them to Moody Blues producer, Denny Cordell. Bolan and Took auditioned and Cordell secured a recording session. Most of the songs from these sessions were old, but 'Debora', chosen as the first single in April 1968, was a recent composition. The new album, *My People Were Fair and Had Sky in Their Hair ... but Now They're Content to Wear*

▶ *Marc Bolan, beloved of English rock fans, was one of the first proponents of Glam Rock and has often been credited with being the 'Godfather of Punk'.*

Stars on Their Brows, was outselling Pink Floyd and Jimi Hendrix by the end of July.

An increasing media profile and industry connections got the band a place in the Blackhill Enterprises management company, and it was here that Bolan met 26 year-old June Child. June left her partner, and the two quickly settled into a flat in Ladbroke Grove in West London. (They married in 1970.) June's presence allowed Bolan's romantic musical phase to bloom. Summer 1968 brought a follow-up single, 'One Inch Rock', taken from the second and shorter-titled album *Prophets, Seers and Sages the Angel of the Ages*. The next album, *Unicorn*, was brought out in May.

In August 1969 Tyrannosaurus Rex set off on their first American tour, but the New York dates coincided with the Woodstock festival upstate. The rest of the tour failed and Bolan returned to Britain without the

▼ *From hippy to 'King of Glam', Marc Bolan went through many changes of style as well as many reverses of fortune. The star was on the verge of a serious comeback when he was tragically killed in a road accident in 1977.*

break he had been expecting. He also returned without Peregrine Took, who had spent most of the tour on acid.

ELECTRIC WARRIOR

In October Bolan found Took's replacement in Mickey Finn, and began to experiment with a more electric sound. *A Beard of Stars* released in March 1970, was the first Bolan album to include the electric guitar.

One of Bolan's most famous singles 'Ride a White Swan', was also written about this time. The band's name was abbreviated to T. Rex, a British tour was organized and they appeared on the television show *Top of the Pops*. New band members Steve Currie and Howard Kaylan arrived.

December brought the release of the album, *T. Rex*. 'Ride a White Swan' went to number 2 as part of its 20-week stay in the top 50 and *T. Rex* reached number 13 in the album charts. The follow-up single 'Hot Love', reached number 1 after a month and stayed there for six weeks. Marc Bolan had hit the big time.

To take the new T. Rex on the road, the band took on drummer Bill Legend whose first gig was in March 1971 in Detroit, on their five-week American tour. Bolan planned a British tour for May, and on it he introduced his audiences to the glitter and sparkle that announced a new Glam movement The single which followed it, 'Get It On', was the second number 1.

Bolan had broken with his hippy past, but was fanning the fervour in his growing teenage following. *Electric Warrior*, the first album for the four-piece T. Rex line-up appeared in September 1971, a month before the start of a British tour which saw the band become the object of mass adulation. The album flew to number 1, and meanwhile the December single release of 'Get It On' in America saw Bolan looking at his first US number 1, and rumoured worldwide sales of 14 million. The distinctive T. Rex sound was consolidated over the next few months with 'Telegram Sam' and 'Metal Guru' both reaching the top of the charts.

UPS AND DOWNS

In February 1972 the band went to America to capitalize on their single success, but again they failed. Worse, Bolan's recent introduction to cocaine caused trouble at Carnegie Hall when he fell over during the first song. Things back home were still going well. With a short but sweet number 1 slot for the re-released double album set of *My People Were Fair* and *Prophets, Seers and Sages*, Bolan was the first to have three number 1 albums in the UK in the same year.

The next album, *The Slider*, appeared in July 1972 and reached number 4, but was slated as 'close to an artistic collapse' by the music critic Charles Shaar Murray. Departures from the Bolan camp followed and he was accused of believing his own publicity material. He had also started to drink heavily under the pressure of another failed American tour.

Christmas 1972 saw the première of Bolan's film project *Born to Boogie* as

▲ *Despite beginning his career in acoustic music, Bolan made the switch to electric sounds which propelled him to stardom and gave him a new nickname among fans: the Electric Warrior.*

well as the release of 'Solid Gold Easy Action', which got to number 2 in the Christmas charts. The film opened to packed houses, and two live London 'Rexmas' shows gave an up-tempo ending to the year.

The beginning of 1973 brought a number 3 slot for '20th Century Boy', but the *Tanx* album did little, while the make-up of the cover photo did not hide the increasingly bloated features of the heavily drinking star. He was letting his image colour his perspective while other Glam musicians were succeeding in the changing market.

By the summer of 1973, Bolan was having an affair with Motown songwriter Gloria Jones, drinking heavily and taking cocaine. Another American tour had failed and the rest of the band was unhappy. Currie and Legend were still making only £50 a week and were increasingly disturbed by Bolan's

erratic behaviour, while Bill Legend left the band in November. By the end of the year June had also made up her mind to leave him.

Bolan set up a flat with Gloria in St John's Wood, London. Planning the first British tour in 18 months, he seemed to be losing control, unable to see beyond his star status. Record production was now formulaic and rows over royalties caused producer Tony Visconti to quit.

Meanwhile Bolan took a break. While Britain bought the Bay City Rollers and Showaddywaddy, he sipped drinks abroad. *Zip Gun*, released in February 1975, was the last T. Rex album to feature Mickey Finn, who left the band that same month, prompting Bolan to comment 'T. Rex no longer exists.'

There was a new career move, however. Television producer Mike Mansfield asked Bolan to appear on his afternoon pop show *Supersonic*, which became his main public outlet. He returned to profile-raising work at the start of 1976, but gigs and a new single 'London Boys' aroused little public interest.

By now Bolan was getting interested in Punk Rock, apparent on the *Dandy in the Underworld* album of spring 1977. His self-proclaimed role as the 'Godfather of Punk' was backed up by Siouxsie and the Banshees' '20th Century Boy'.

Bolan's drive towards stability continued with the purchase of a new house, while the final *Supersonic* in March 1977 was succeeded by a monthly column for the *Record Mirror*. He also jumped at Mike Mansfield's proposal for a new television programme which would become the six-episode *Marc*. The series provided a platform and gave him the chance to feature new bands.

The final programme climaxed with the first live performance of Bolan and David Bowie.

A LEGEND DIES

On 16 September Bolan went to the Speakeasy Club and then on to Morton's restaurant with Gloria and some friends. Leaving at about 4 am, he and Gloria drove off in her purple Mini 1275 GT. At about 5 am, the car crashed into a tree on a bend just past the hump-back bridge on Queen's Ride, on the edge of Barnes Common in south-west London. Gloria was badly injured, but the passenger side had taken the brunt of the collision. Marc Bolan was dead.

Marc Bolan's funeral was held at Golders Green crematorium, attended by a crowd of family, friends, associates and fans.

▼ *From his very earliest days, Bolan was always image-conscious; in fact he had the ambition to be a star – of some kind – even before his talent for music propelled him to dizzy heights.*

The Busby Babes

Young lives cut short

6 February 1958

At three minutes past three on the afternoon of Thursday 6 February 1958, Commander James Thain, chief pilot of a British European Airways Elizabethan 609 turbo-prop airliner, prepared for take-off after a refuelling stop at Munich's Riem Airport. Ahead of him stretched the ice-cold, slush-strewn runway, a concrete strip down which he and his co-pilot, Captain Ken Rayment, had already powered the Elizabethan twice that day in failed attempts to begin the flight to Manchester, home destination of his passengers. On both occasions, they had experienced a sudden and completely incomprehensible drop in engine thrust.

Now, after technicians had checked the aircraft, Thain confirmed his intention to proceed. As the Elizabethan accelerated along the runway, Thain and Rayment watched in horror as the needle on the speed indicator suddenly and inexplicably dropped from a satisfactory 117 knots to a mere 105 – not enough to effect take-off. Less than a minute later, the aircraft lay in a field, its fuselage ripped apart into two separate segments. Only 21 of the 44 people on board would survive.

This was a disaster, not merely for the families and friends of those either killed or fatally injured in the crash, but also for the untold thousands of sports fans for whom many of the casualties were idols, young Titans of the game of football. These were the remarkable Busby Babes, the young Manchester United team with an average

age of only 22, painstakingly created by the visionary former Manchester City player Matt Busby out of the ruins of World War II.

Busby had become manager of Manchester United in October 1945, after returning from military service to civilian life. With an unprecedented five-year contract, he began the job of rebuilding the club. It was a formidable task. The

> ## A team and a dream died, but the legend still lives on at Old Trafford

club's Old Trafford ground was still a tangled heap of wreckage, thanks to direct hits by German bombs in 1941, so that United had to use Maine Road, Manchester City's ground during the rebuilding. The club was also a hefty £15,000 in debt. The squad he inherited was a solid one, however, and certainly a firm enough foundation on which to start building a team capable of matching his vision. Busby also brought in Jimmy

Murphy, a former West Bromwich and Wales player he had met during the war, to be the assistant manager.

Within three years of his taking over the management, the club won the FA (Football Association) Cup, and in 1951-52, secured the League Championship for the first time in 41 years.

THE BIRTH OF THE BABES

In the wake of the League Championship season, Busby decided that the veterans in his squad had to be replaced. Good and loyal as they were, many were ready to be transferred to other teams, move on into coaching jobs or simply hang up their boots. He quickly enlarged United's network of trusted scouts to help him find youngsters with high potential who could be moulded into the kind of players Busby and Murphy could use to take the club to greater victories. Once taken on, these youngsters were coaxed and groomed by coach Bert Whalley and trainer Tom Curry. The 'Busby Babes' had arrived, though no one had yet coined their unforgettable nickname.

The new wingers Busby signed were Bolton's Harry McShane and Johnny Berry, a Birmingham City player who had impressed Busby a year earlier. United also acquired a new outside left – the 20-year-old Roger Byrne. Byrne began his first team career at left back, but was then switched to left wing for the last six games of the season. As the first graduate of

▲ *The ill-fated team line up on the pitch before the start of their match with Red Star in Belgrade. With no premonition of the disaster about to happen, their only worry is the final score.*

Busby's innovative youth training academy, he was the first true Busby Babe.

When United depressingly lost six of their first 11 games in the 1952–53 season, Busby knew he had to act fast, acquire new players on the open market and bring on some of the youngsters that his scouts had brought to the club in preceding years. The transfer market yielded the talents of Tommy Taylor, a strong and combative centre forward bought from Barnsley. Roger Byrne's new team-mate at right back was Bill Foulkes.

However, this season would go down in history as the one in which the most famous Busby Babe of all – left half Duncan Edwards – made his transition from the youth squad to the first team.

Taken into the United fold when he was still a growing boy of 14, Edwards formed a a memorable and formidable mid-field partnership with Eddie 'Snake Hips' Colman at right half and centre half Mark Jones. His debut, against Cardiff City at Old Trafford on Easter Monday, 1953, was achieved at the incredibly young age of 15 years, 285 days.

By the beginning of the 1952–53 season, Manchester United's regular goal-keeping duties had already been given to another youngster as Ray Wood replaced Reg Allen. With Tommy Taylor all-conquering at centre forward, the arrival of local boy Dennis Viollet in 1953 gave Matt Busby a front-line double act which proved unrivalled in the English league. David Pegg, recruited from Doncaster, became left winger. In that year, which also saw the regular first team blooding of Ulsterman Jackie Blanchflower, brother of Tottenham Hotspur's double-winning captain Danny,

and 20-year-old Jeff Whitefoot, United achieved fourth spot in the Championship.

In 1954-55, United finished the season in fifth place, and in the following season regained the League Championship. When they retained the title in 1956–57, the team went an unparalleled step further with a season goal tally of 103, with two newcomers – the teenagers Bobby Charlton and Billy Whelan – scoring 10 and 26 respectively.

EUROPE

The Busby Babes' first excursion into Europe came in the 1956–57 season, when their League Championship win of the season before qualified them for participation in the relatively new but prestigious European Cup. The first English club to

▲ *Ten-year-old memories of the tragedy in Munich and thoughts of what might have been must have haunted Sir Matt Busby in the months before the 1968 European Cup Final.*

Taylor added 3 of his own, Billy Whelan put 2 in, and Johnny Berry slotted another into the net to make the final scoreline an extraordinary and more than convincing 10-1.

The next round found the unstoppable United up against the West German champions Borussia Dortmund. At home, on 17 October, United achieved a 3–2 win – enough to ensure they would be put into the last eight when the November away game ended in a goal-less draw.

The quarter-finals saw United pitched against Spain's Athletico Bilbao. Drawn away in the first leg in January 1957, United ended the disappointing game with a 2-goal deficit. In the home leg game on 6 February, the helpless Bilboans found themselves under repeated attack as Busby's Babes regained their form, fought for, and scored, the vital three goals they needed to stay in Europe.

United now looked ahead to their first semi-final meeting with European Cup-holders Real Madrid on 11 April 1957. If the prospect of facing the awesome might of a Real Madrid team, which featured the likes of superstar centre forward and captain Alfredo di Stafano, and deadly strikers like Gento, Mateos and Kopa, was not enough to intimidate the United squad, Real's vast Bernabeu Stadium was every bit as awe-inspiring – tier upon tier of seats, every one of them occupied, with 120,000 hysterical fans who made the roar of an Old Trafford crowd sound like the

murmur of a gentleman's club lounge. The challenge proved too much, and United found themselves out-run, out-passed and frankly out-classed from the off as Real drove home the lesson.

A SECOND CHANCE

It was a subdued bunch of Babes who returned to England and the reality of League football. Unable to beat Real Madrid at Maine Road on 25 April, United found themselves out of the European Cup with a 3–5 aggregate score. But they at least had the satisfaction of knowing that their League title, which they had retained, guaranteed that they would be playing in Europe once more.

Their first European encounter of the 1957-58 season, on 25 September, saw an on-form United travel to the Republic of Ireland to begin the demolition of local League champions, Shamrock Rovers,

▼ *Matt Busby, Pat Crerand and George Best start the journey home to Old Trafford with a trophy of special significance to players past and present after winning the European Cup in May 1968.*

play for the Cup, they were drawn against the Belgian champions Anderlecht in the first round. United travelled to Brussels in September 1956, where goals from Dennis Viollet and Tommy Taylor made them 2–1 victors in the first leg. It was a confident start from a side who came to be nicknamed 'The Red Devils', because of their red shirts, by admiring Europeans.

That admiration quickly turned to awe when the two teams met again at Maine Road, the Manchester City ground, two weeks later (Old Trafford's floodlighting system was still not fully operational), and the Belgians were smashed out of the tournament by a fantastic goal blitz. During 90 minutes which a dazed Matt Busby described as 'the greatest thrill in a lifetime of soccer', Viollet scored 4 goals, which ensured that the English team went comfortably through to a second round meeting with the much stronger and more formidable Czech champions, Dukla Prague, on 21 November.

Despite winning the first home leg game against Dukla Prague 3–0, the Babes lost the return game in Prague 0–1 on 4 December. Still, they once again had the heartening prospect of playing at home for the first of their two quarter-final matches against the Yugoslavian champions, Red Star Belgrade.

On 14 January 1958, United emerged 2–1 victors in a tight, demanding and exciting game against Red Star which made it very clear that the second leg, to be played in Belgrade on 5 February, was going to be a tough one.

THE LAST MATCH

Busby's young stars departed for Belgrade, and Roger Byrne took the field as skipper of the already legendary team that Red Star's fans were desperate to see in action. United took the lead in just two minutes, and 20 minutes into the game they were 2–0 up, courtesy of a Bobby Charlton thunderbolt. Astonishingly, the stadium erupted in a riot of sound as massive numbers of Red Star supporters began cheering every tricky move, every remarkable display of skill that the phenomenal Babes used to bewilder the home team. Just before half-time, Charlton beat Red Star's keeper Beara with another 25-yard screamer.

Whatever Red Star's coach said to his men in the dressing room, it obviously worked. They came out firing on all cylinders, making the score 3–1 two minutes later. Red Star launched attack after attack, with United's defence stretched time and again.

In the Manchester United dressing room after the game, there was disappointment at having let a 3–0 lead slip to a 3–3 draw. But there was elation, too, in knowing that this was still enough to put them through, once again, to the European Cup semi-finals and a meeting with the Italian

superstars of AC Milan. No one could guess that the game against Red Star would be the Babes' last.

THE SHOCK AND THE GRIEF

Only when the rescue teams began rushing in to help after the crash occurred, just a day after Belgrade, did the full horror of the situation became clear. Seven players, Geoff Bent, David Pegg, Mark Jones, Eddie Colman, Tommy Taylor, Billy Whelan and Roger Byrne, had been killed outright. Only 28 years old when he died, Byrne had not even learned the news that he was going to become a father for the first time. His widow Joy would give birth to a son, Roger, eight months after the crash. Club secretary Walter Crickman was also killed outright, as were Tom Curry, the first team trainer, and coach Bert Whalley. Many respected sports journalists lost their lives too.

Johnny Berry and Duncan Edwards were left fighting for their lives. So, too, was the flight's co-pilot, Ken Rayment. Two weeks after the crash, when doctors were just starting to think he might possibly pull through, Edwards finally succumbed to his injuries, aged 21. Rayment also died, his body unable to deal with the trauma of

▲ *Fans, Mancunians and much of the nation were stunned by the news of the devastating aircrash in which nine players of one of the most exciting young teams in football history died.*

being crushed by wreckage. For a long while it was feared that Matt Busby would also die, his chest crushed and a foot broken by the impact.

Johnny Berry and Jackie Blanchflower eventually recovered from their injuries but were unable to resume their playing careers, while Albert Scanlon, Dennis Viollet, Ken Morgans, Bobby Charlton and Ray Wood all played their part in reshaping Manchester United's future.

In the wake of the disaster, the road to recovery was a long one, but finally, on 29 May 1968, United beat Benfica 4–1 at Wembley and at last held the European Cup in their hands. Those who survived to share this triumph had every reason to reflect on what might have been, and remember the friends they had lost at Munich ten years earlier.

Karen Carpenter

Singer with a sad secret

1950–1983

Agnes Carpenter and her husband, Harold moved into their house in New Haven, Connecticut, in August 1946. Their first child, Richard Lynne, was born soon after. Three and half years later, on 2 March 1950, his parents presented him with a sister, Karen Anne Carpenter.

Harold and Agnes were music-lovers and fostered Richard's musical inclinations from a very early age. Karen, meanwhile, was a more active, extrovert child, but her admiration of her brother often led her to join him in his appreciation of music.

Richard's piano lessons began his practical musical training, and by the time he was 12 his talent was apparent. A year later, he passed an audition for the Yale Music School. At 15 he was in demand with local groups. Shortly after, he cut his first record as pianist for a local band, The Barries.

In June 1963 the family moved to Downey, California, a suburb of Los Angeles. Karen missed her friends, and it must have been hard watching the progress of her brother, who was now performing in a jazz band.

Soon, however, she discovered the drums and was sharing Richard's achievements. Her first public appearance, though, was singing in a competition, which Richard had entered with an original song. There they met Wes Jacobs, teamed up and began playing as the Richard Carpenter Trio. Karen came across as an oddity – a girl who sang *and* played the drums.

The trio progressed swiftly, appearing in a 'Battle of the Bands' held at the Hollywood Bowl in June 1966. Richard recruited a guitarist, bass player and vocalist, and they played under the name of Spectrum. Only after the demise of Spectrum did Richard and Karen go into the recording studio. They were happy with the new sound and it proved itself at an audition for the television talent programme *Your All American College Show*, for which they called themselves, simply, Carpenters.

A body and a life destroyed by the cruel tragedy of obsessive dieting and anorexia

Then the duo had a stroke of luck: their demo found its way to Herb Alpert, one of the founders of A&M Records. He liked the sound, and on 22 April 1969, 22-year-old Richard and 19-year-old Karen signed a contract with A&M and began work on an album. Entitled *Offering*, it was ready for release in October 1969. The first single, a cover of the Beatles' 'Ticket To Ride', reached a respectable number 54.

The next single, a double 'A'-side, with an arrangement of Burt Bacharach's 'They Long To Be Close To You', was an instant hit, going to number 1 in America. The follow-up album, *Close To You*, was recorded and packaged as fast as possible, and went on to sell five million copies. At the 1970 Grammy awards, Richard and Karen reaped two awards: best new artist and best contemporary vocal group.

Their fans' enthusiasm was not shared by the critics, who took exception to stars who insisted on being average people. The criticism was centred upon their personal style and their clean living.

In reality, the workload and the pressures of the music business made it impossible to be 'normal' people. The family unit that Richard and Karen made out of their entourage, numbering as many as 30 people, separated them from the outside world. In any case, the duo rarely had time for outside contacts since they were on the road for most of the five years from 1970.

The continual touring tested the unity of the band. Mistakes could also bring a harsh reprimand from either Richard or Karen, as they insisted on studio tracks being note-perfect in performance. They

▶ *Karen Carpenter on stage, sadly revealing the serious effects of the compulsive dieting which eventually contributed to her tragic death.*

were as hard on each other as they were on the other band members, regularly arguing over details. Karen's need to be in control extended to dissatisfaction with her body. She made use of various slimming devices to keep her weight at the level that previous dieting had accomplished.

FIRST WARNINGS

About 1974, Karen's friends and family started to notice her irregular eating habits, realizing that she had lost much of her full figure. Turning 25, Karen was the first to admit that she had much to be thankful for, but she also felt inadequate. No amount of praise from friends or colleagues could dispel her feeling that she had won success under false pretences. She was also still alone, since her stated requirements for a partner seemed extremely difficult to fulfil. In the person of Terry Ellis, however, her needs seemed to be satisfied.

Meanwhile, the music continued to flow. The next batch of singles came from the *Horizon* album of June 1975, the seventh in six years. But the success was putting increasing strain on the pair. Neither Karen nor Richard was in the best of condition. He was becoming more and more reliant on sleeping pills while Karen's growing obsession with reducing her weight was making her look gaunt.

Yet another tour brought them even closer to breaking point by their choice of support act – Neil Sedaka. Richard was so desperate about being upstaged that in August 1975 he sacked Sedaka. The press had a field day, for Sedaka claimed that he had been fired because he was too good.

The whole Carpenters' 'family' was jolted and their manager was sacked. Terry Ellis agreed to take over temporarily, but he was too late to save the tour. Karen in any case was now down to about 80 pounds and was ordered into hospital.

Karen was allowed home after a short time. Though still weak, she had recovered somewhat by October, and she and Ellis took a holiday before resuming life in Los

Angeles, although they both knew that there were insurmountable differences between them. Karen returned, distraught, to the house she shared with Richard, feeling that she would never find anyone as right for her as Ellis.

'A Kind Of Hush (All Over The World)' was the only hit single from the album *Kind of Hush* that the Carpenters released in 1976. They had been considering a change of direction and earlier in the year had signed Jerry Weintraub as their manager. Along with Karen's family and the band, he soon became aware of her state of health. Everyone tried to make her recognize she had a problem, but she had become single-minded about reaching a dangerously low target weight.

MOUNTING PRESSURES

The 1977 album release was a further source of worry for the duo, as they wanted to regain the form they felt they had lost over the past two records. It did not realize their hopes and was the first not to go 'gold'. For Richard and Karen, who had spent years concentrating on their music, the loss of sales was very worrying. The additional pressure hit their weakened dispositions hard. Richard's intake of sleeping pills was causing serious physical problems. He admitted his dependency and began a two-year battle to free himself of the addiction.

Richard reached his lowest ebb on tour in September 1978 when he realized he couldn't continue with the live shows. His playing was suffering from the effects of the sleeping-pills, and he was terrified of cracking up on stage. He and Karen paid off the band, not guessing that, aged 31 and 28 respectively, they had played the last concert of their joint careers.

Karen flew to London for a promotional commitment at the end of 1978, with the

▲ *The Carpenters early in their career. During the early seventies the duo and their group toured and recorded relentlessly. The pressure of this workload would soon began to tell on both of them.*

excuse that Richard had 'flu. He knew that he was useless to the partnership as well as himself, and booked himself into a Kansas treatment centre in January 1979.

Karen visited him after a couple of weeks, in the middle of the initial, most difficult period of withdrawal. There were angry exchanges, as he tried to get Karen to admit to her problem, including the dreaded words 'anorexia nervosa'. She at last agreed to have some hospital checks.

Even so, Karen seemed more concerned with the offer of a solo venture with producer Phil Ramone. She flew to New York for initial meetings with Ramone and work began in mid-1979 after Karen had taken up residence in a hotel for the duration of the recording.

The pressure of working with someone

other than Richard began to tell. At one point Ramone found her passed out on her hotel-room floor. She admitted to taking the same sleeping pill that had got Richard in so much trouble. She did *not* admit that she was also taking thyroid medication to speed up her metabolism. For an anorexic to put strain on her heart on top of the strain caused by lack of food was extremely dangerous.

After finishing the recording, Karen was ready to go back to the studio with Richard, but he refused until she regained some weight. The threat worked. She saw a specialist who brought her weight up to over 100 pounds. She was happy and positive in the spring of 1980 and even submitted to a blind date organized by one of her friends, and so met Tom Burris.

Burris was charming and the two fell head over heels in love. They were engaged in

▼ *Richard and Karen at the height of their fame. Their stage show and presentation may have become much more expensive and sophisticated, but the physical toll taken by all those years of compulsive work is all too obvious in both of them. This is the real price of fame.*

two months. The summer wedding took place in Beverley Hills. While they were on honeymoon, Richard prepared material for what he hoped would be the 1981 comeback album, *Made In America*. Its content promised a new, positive mood.

The news of Karen's marriage, however, was not so heartening. Tom Burris's adventurous view of life was more than the homeloving Karen could handle. He walked out of the Carpenter house in November 1981, never to see Karen again.

DESPERATE CONDITION

Part of the problem must have been Karen's realization that she had to do something about her health. In October 1981, desperate enough to seek help, she worked up the courage to ring Dr Steven Levenkron, an authority on eating disorders. He said that he could only help her if she came to New York. In November, she flew to meet him.

A 31-year-old woman taking thyroid tablets and laxatives, Karen weighed 78 pounds. Levenkron worked at breaking down her drug dependency, and talked about her feelings of conflict. She stopped

▲ *Karen Carpenter signed her first recording contract at the age of nineteen. By the age of twenty-five she was at the peak of her career, and one of the most successful popular singers in the world; but by that time she had also begun to diet non-stop, taking the terrible risks with her health which would cause her tragically early death in 1983.*

using laxatives for a while and her weight went up, but she soon relapsed and looked as thin as when she first arrived.

She left the hospital after two months in November 1982, weighing 90 pounds. Back in Los Angeles it was clear that Karen was not on the road to recovery, despite her protestations to the contrary.

At the beginning of 1983, Karen was in high spirits, looking forward to working. She visited her mother and they discussed buying clothes. She stayed overnight as she regularly did. In the morning, Agnes found her collapsed in the bedroom. It was 4 February 1983. Her heart had given up. The autopsy report gave the cause of death as heart failure due to anorexia nervosa.

Karen Carpenter was buried four days later. Her coffin contained Tom Burris's wedding ring. The inscription on the marble crypt read:
KAREN 1950–1983. A STAR ON EARTH. A STAR IN HEAVEN.

Kurt Cobain

Grunge generation hero

1967–1994

On 5 April 1994, Kurt Cobain blew his head off. The body was discovered on 8 April. The police had to use fingerprints for a positive I.D.; dental records were no use.

Kurt's story began on 20 February 1967 in the small town of Aberdeen in Washington State, where there is little but trailer parks and logging yards. His father Donald was a mechanic while his mother Wendy kept home in the house the Cobains bought in Aberdeen six months after Kurt was born.

It was a stable home until, at the age of seven, Kurt's idyllic childhood ended. His parents' marriage failed, and their divorce changed him completely. He became withdrawn and moody. For a year or so, he stayed with his mother and sister, but took against his mother's new boyfriend and ran wild. Eventually Wendy lost patience and sent him off to live with Don.

In 1978, however, Don remarried and Kurt found himself with a stepmother and stepbrother. He felt betrayed and took violently against his stepmother. He began to cut school. At home he refused to do chores and picked on his stepbrother. Don's response was to beat him.

Kurt's one refuge was in music. He got a secondhand electric guitar for his fourteenth birthday and took a week's lessons, learning how to play AC/DC's 'Back in Black'. He moved on to 'Louie Louie' and 'Another One Bites the Dust'. He also began to write his own stuff.

If there were bands in Aberdeen, they were cover bands, apart from the Melvins. Kurt became devoted to them, going to every gig and helping with equipment. In August 1984 Black Flag played the Mountaineer Club in Seattle. Kurt drove up with the Melvins for the gig. He came back, spiked his hair and decided to form a band.

Meanwhile he was thrown out again by his mother, and lasted only a week with his

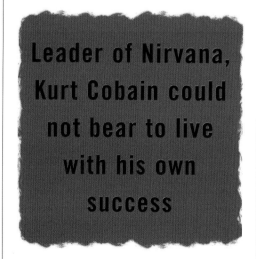

Leader of Nirvana, Kurt Cobain could not bear to live with his own success

father. He also flunked school in May 1985, just before graduation. He got a job and rented an apartment in Aberdeen, but he was soon evicted. During the winter of 1985 he slept rough under the North Aberdeen Bridge. Another part of Kurt's new life was drugs. That summer he took heroin for the first time.

Guilty about her son's homelessness Wendy helped Kurt out with the deposit

an apartment, but he was soon evicted. Meanwhile he had started going out with Tracy Marander. They met at a punk club in Seattle and when he was evicted he moved into her studio flat in Olympia.

NIRVANA – THE EARLY DAYS

Desperate to earn money, Kurt started a cover band, to play in local redneck bars. In fact, it never played, but did mark the first tie-up between Kurt and Chris Novoselic, with whom he would eventually form Nirvana.

The two persevered with the band though, getting Aaron Burckhard in to play drums. From late 1987 on, they began to get a following. They had not settled on a name, playing variously as Skid Row, Throat Oyster, and Windowpane. They then tried Bliss before hitting on Nirvana. They still had drummer trouble. Three drummers came and went in just under a year, before they finally found the one they thought they were looking for in Chad Channing.

By January 1988, Kurt and Chris had enough money to make a demo. They went to Reciprocal Recordings, the

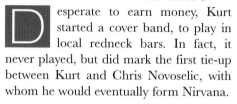

▶ **Kurt Cobain, leader of the band Nirvana, and writer of songs that would inspire his generation. The last words of his suicide note read, 'So remember it's better to burn out than to fade away,' a quote from Neil Young song which mourned the loss of Elvis.**

Cobain with his wife Courtney Love and their daughter Frances. Because of the couple's heroin addiction, Frances was taken from them by the LA authorities after her birth. It was only after months of persuasion that they got the child back – not that the experience did anything to wean the pair off drugs.

broken-down studio of Jack Endino, house producer for Sub Pop records. For $152 they laid down and mixed ten songs in six hours. Endino liked the tape and made a remix for Jonathan Poneman of Sub Pop. Excited by the tape, Poneman got in touch and a deal was agreed for Sub Pop to put out Nirvana's first record, which eventually came out in November.

Encouraged by its success, Nirvana started rehearsing songs for what was to become their first album, *Bleach*. Sub Pop said they

had no money. Despite this, Kurt booked a studio with Endino. They started recording on Christmas Eve and by early January had finished the ten tracks. The album cost $606 to record.

Following the release of *Bleach* in June 1989, Nirvana went on their first US tour – with no road crew, no one to sort out where they were going to eat or sleep. They played tiny venues and often hardly anyone turned up. Later in the year they went to Europe. Starting in Britain in Newcastle, they played 36 shows in 42 days. Although they played to big crowds, the gigs were a strain. Kurt spent most of the tour drunk or asleep. By the time they reached Rome, he was ready to snap. Four songs into the set he smashed his guitar, walked off stage and climbed a speaker stack, threatening to jump, before he set off hand over hand across the rafters, screaming at the audience below.

As well as playing on his nerves, Kurt's long absences on tour had put a strain on his relationship with Tracy. Halfway through the second US tour in April 1990 he called from Amherst, Massachusetts, to say he was moving out.

FAME AND FORTUNE

Kurt had been writing songs towards Nirvana's second album. In April 1990 they made a first recording of the new material with Butch Vig at his studio in Wisconsin. The session revealed the shortcomings in Chad's drumming. When they came back to Seattle Chad was fired and Nirvana turned to David Grohl as replacement.

As bootleg copies of the sessions with Butch Vig circulated, Nirvana were pursued by the major record labels, finally opting for the Geffen label. The deal was not sealed until April 1991. Through the winter the band stayed in Seattle. Kurt and Dave shared the flat in Olympia. Kurt had black memories of the period: music and heroin were his only consolation.

In April 1991, the band began recording the new album with Butch Vig in Los Angeles. The climate and working on the new record brought a change in mood. Also Kurt did not know any dealers in LA so he was off the heroin, although he drank codeine cough syrup constantly.

When the album, later called *Nevermind*, was finished, everyone was pleased with it, but they wouldn't find out exactly how good it was until 'Smells Like Teen Spirit' was released in September. As a result, the summer of 1991 found them optimistic and confident. Kurt had another reason for feeling good. He had started to see Courtney Love.

In September 1991 *Nevermind* was released, with 'Smells Like Teen Spirit' as the first single. No one was prepared for its impact. It opened at 144 on the Billboard chart; by December it had reached number 1, selling over 300,000 copies a week.

▼ *Seen from the outside Kurt Cobain really did have everything: fame, money, a wife who loved him, and a young daughter. None of it, though, would prevent him from turning his back on it all and taking his own life with a shotgun in April 1994.*

Nirvana's lives were transformed. On the autumn tour of the States, they found their audience made up of mainly heavy metal kids and Guns 'n' Roses fans. The change did not agree with Kurt. After the US tour they went to Europe. Kurt was becoming disillusioned and bored with touring. So he turned to Courtney – her band Hole were on tour in Europe at the same time. She met Kurt in Amsterdam where the two turned to heroin. In December, when the Nirvana tour ended, Kurt went back to Seattle and started doing heroin daily.

BITTER JOYS

After Christmas 1991 Dave and Chris noticed that something was wrong: Kurt's moods were erratic, his behaviour unreliable. They saw less and less of him. It was at this time that Courtney discovered she was pregnant. With their most recent US tour ending in Hawaii, Kurt and Courtney decided to get married. The ceremony took place on a cliff above a beach on 24 February 1992.

From early 1992 the press had scented a story in Kurt and Courtney. In September *Vanity Fair* magazine carried an interview with Courtney, in which she detailed her drugs binge with Kurt in New York, and the apparent admission that she had taken heroin when she knew she was pregnant.

The world was convinced that the pair were junkies and that the baby would be deformed. In this they were disappointed: a healthy daughter was born on 18 August. Still the LA County Department of Child Services moved in. The couple had to surrender custody of Frances Bean to Courtney's sister. By the end of the year, however, they had managed to persuade the authorities that Frances should be allowed to live with them.

Meanwhile, Kurt was preparing songs for a new album. It was now 18 months since they had finished *Nevermind* and the time was right for another album. Grunge had become mainstream and the whole thing dismayed Kurt. He was determined to make a record to challenge the audience gathered from *Nevermind*.

In February 1993, they went to Steve Albini's studio in Minnesota and recorded everything in six days. The management at Geffen hated it, although in the end only two tracks, 'Heart-shaped Box' and 'All Apologies', were much changed.

When *In Utero* was released in September, it may have come as a surprise to discover how listenable it was. But this could not hide the bitter rage in the lyrics, as Kurt took his chance to have his say on the events since *Nevermind*. Nirvana were now established MTV darlings and the perceived standard bearers of the indie scene. Kurt could not escape; he had become the kind of rock star he had always despised, but what his audience wanted and what Geffen were intent to give them was Nirvana.

PRIVATE PAIN

All that October and November, they toured the States. The band were playing well, having added a second guitarist, Pat Smear, to the line-up. Kurt was in good form, off heroin since May, but the long periods of separation from Courtney and Frances Bean made him remote and abstracted. After Christmas the tour moved to Europe. All went well until the end of February but then Kurt just seemed to come to a halt. He played badly in Milan and again in Germany. Finally after a concert on 1 March in Munich, he declared he had had enough and would not play again.

He flew to Rome. Courtney and Frances flew from London to meet him, but this was not enough to lift his mood. It is not clear what happened, but on 3 March he attempted suicide. Courtney found him in a drug-induced coma beside a suicide note the following morning. He was rushed to hospital and made a full recovery.

The couple returned to Seattle on 10 March and all seemed fine. According to the record company, Nirvana would later

▲ *Kurt on stage about a year before his death, during one of the promotional tours for what would be Nirvana's final studio album* In Utero.

play the cancelled European dates. In fact, Kurt was hurtling to self-destruction. He was sighted in his old heroin haunts. Courtney feared they would lose Frances again. Threatened with divorce, he joined her in a rehabilitation programme, but discharged himself after three days. He returned to Seattle and bought a shotgun, claiming he needed it for self-defence.

Kurt then disappeared. Desperate, Courtney looked for him in LA, hired private detectives to search Seattle and rang his mother and all his friends. On 5 April he returned to his mansion in Lake Washington Boulevard. He shot up with heroin and valium, put the shotgun in his mouth and squeezed the trigger with his toe. He was 27 years old.

James Dean

Rebel without a cause

1931–1955

James Byron Dean was born on 8 February 1931 in Fairmount, Indiana. His parents both came from families that had farmed in the area for generations. His father, Winton Dean, was the first to break away from his heritage and had become a dental technician. His mother, Mildred Wilson, had married Winton after a brief courtship when she discovered she was pregnant.

When Jimmy was five, his father was transferred to the Sawtelle Veterans Administration in Los Angeles and the family moved to Santa Monica. Four years later his mother died of cancer.

Unable to leave his job in Los Angeles, Winton sought help from his family to look after his son. His uncle and aunt, Marcus and Ortense Winslow, volunteered. Conservative, God-fearing folk, they brought Jimmy up to follow their beliefs.

Jimmy was an adventurous child and remained so throughout his short life. Despite his short sight, he was given to trying tricks on the trapeze, while his talent for physical and verbal mimicry came out at an early age. On his thirteenth birthday Marcus gave him a moped with which Jimmy began his affair with speed that was eventually to kill him.

As he grew older, home life at the farm became duller, and Jimmy's ideas and aspirations began moving away from the Winslows. He developed an infatuation for Dr James DeWeerd, the pastor of the

Wesleyan Church in Fairmount. He introduced Jimmy to the world of ideas, and also to the world of homosexuality.

During his school days, Jimmy appeared in virtually all the plays that were put on, making a great impression. The time came for him to leave, though. Against Marcus Winslow's wishes, Winton Dean decided that Jimmy should study in California. In June 1949 he left for Los Angeles.

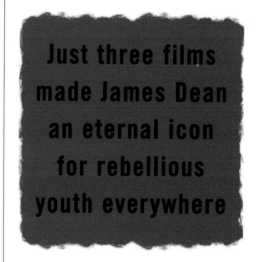

Just three films made James Dean an eternal icon for rebellious youth everywhere

Jimmy went to live with his father and his second wife, Ethel Case. Their relationship was not happy and they argued about his choice of career. A lot of drama options were offered at Santa Monica and, despite his father's objections, Jimmy entered as many courses as he could. After a period at Santa Monica it became clear that Jimmy was doing well in his studies, and he was able to persuade a reluctant Winton that he should study drama at UCLA. In

October, after a week of auditions for UCLA's major productions, Jimmy got the part of Malcolm in *Macbeth*.

NEW YORK

While training, Jimmy started a series of odd jobs, such as car parking at the CBS radio station. Soon after this began, he met Rogers Brackett, an advertising executive who directed his own shows, and who was part of the Hollywood homosexual scene. Jimmy moved in with Brackett, who got him work on radio shows, as well as one-liner roles in Sam Fuller's film *Fixed Bayonets*, and in the Dean Martin/Jerry Lewis film *Sailor Beware*. This wasn't enough for an ambitious young actor, however, increasingly in despair about the quantity and quality of his work, and Jimmy left college to study under James Whitmore, film star and Broadway actor. Whitmore advised him that if he really wanted to learn acting he should go to New York and study under Elia Kazan, who ran the Actors' Studio.

New York was the hub of television production in the 1950s and there was a constant demand for actors. Jimmy got an agent, Jane Deacy, and in November, two months after he had arrived, a job testing stunts on a show called *Beat the Clock*.

▶ *A studio publicity shot for James Dean, the young actor who was to epitomize teenage rebellion in the 1950s.*

Jimmy met and moved in with Elizabeth 'Dizzy' Sheridan, a dancer, but the pair drifted apart when Rogers Brackett moved to New York. Jimmy was broke and the lure of rent-free living outweighed his romance. Brackett was a useful contact and several bit parts came Jimmy's way in early 1952 – acting rather than stunts.

Through Brackett Jimmy had met Lemuel Ayers, a theatrical producer, who offered him a part in the stage play *See the Jaguar*: the role of a 16-year-old totally cut off from the world by an over-protective mother. Apparently, the author, N. Richard Nash, thought Jimmy perfect for the part, that of someone lost in and confused by the world.

In November he finally auditioned for Elia Kazan, then at the height of his career as a

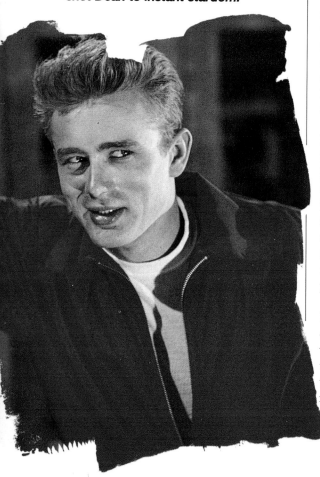

▼ **Rebel Without a Cause *was James Dean's second movie. Based on the lives of teenage gang members, it struck a nerve with the alienated American youth of the mid-fifties, and shot Dean to instant stardom.***

director. Jimmy and a friend Christine White were accepted for the Actors' Studio. On 3 December 1952 *See the Jaguar* opened and the cast awaited the reviews at Sardi's restaurant. Jimmy was a delighted centre of attention, but unfortunately, the play was panned and withdrawn after five performances.

See the Jaguar, however, put some money in his pocket, enabling him to indulge his love of speed: he bought an Indian 500 motorcycle. More television roles came his way because of reviews of his performance in *See the Jaguar*, though he was often cast as a psychotic, which gives some idea of how directors saw him – moody and difficult. He thought himself above learning technique, and liked to act in his own way.

REBELLION

His next big stage part was in an adaptation of André Gide's novel *The Immoralist*. The pre-Broadway run was in Philadelphia, where it was very well received. It was seen one night by Paul Osborn, who was writing the screenplay for *East of Eden*. Impressed, he recommended that Elia Kazan see the play when it moved to New York.

The Immoralist was not well received by the critics; but the first night audience went wild, especially the gay element. Instead of taking a bow, Jimmy curtsied, incensing the director Daniel Mann. Jimmy responded by giving two weeks' notice.

▲ *This is the famous – or infamous – silver Porsche Spyder 550 in which the young star, driving to a race meeting in Salinas, met his death on Route 466.*

THE MAKING OF A STAR

Jimmy was lucky that Elia Kazan saw *The Immoralist* despite his short time in it. Kazan thought Jimmy might be right for the part of Cal in *East of Eden*. He chose him because: 'He has a grudge against all fathers. He is vengeful; he has a sense of aloneness and of being persecuted.'

The budget for *East of Eden* was large by 1954 standards – $1,600,000 – as it was to be shot in CinemaScope, a big-screen format, in colour. None of the crew could believe that Jimmy – a scruffy, short, bespectacled youth – was to be the star. Shooting began on 26 May.

Jimmy received $300 a week until the contract was signed and with his new-found wealth, he bought a motorbike, a Triumph T-110, which he drove around the studio, much to the annoyance of Kazan, who was not keen on Jimmy's apparent death wish, nor the threat it posed to others on the lot. Kazan banned Jimmy from riding the motorcycle until the film was finished, so Jimmy bought himself an MG TA, just to satisfy his lust for speed.

The biggest romance of Jimmy's life started at this time. The object of his love was Pier Angeli, a 22-year-old actress from Sardinia. Though devoted to begin with, their relationship became increasingly tempestuous. He was living on the lot next to Kazan, who often heard the couple rowing, after which Jimmy would get drunk. He had a strong self-destructive streak. The couple eventually split.

On 4 January 1955, it was announced that Jimmy had been signed for *Rebel Without a Cause*, which was to be directed by Nicolas Ray. On 18 January production meetings began, and shortly afterwards Jimmy and Nick Ray visited New York, to look for other members of the cast. While he was there Jimmy was also signed by Warner for the part of Jett Rink in *Giant*, to be directed by George Stevens. He left New York, on 7 March, the eve of the première preview of *East of Eden* in Times Square, saying he 'couldn't handle that scene'. *Rebel* was due to begin filming at the end of March.

The plot of *Rebel* centred on teenage gangs, alienated from unloving or absent parents, trying to find their own identity; Jimmy was almost typecast. The extras included a real gang leader to make sure that the action was authentic. However, all the teenagers had to be shorter than Jimmy — less than 5 feet 8 inches (1.7 metres)!

A LOVE AFFAIR WITH SPEED

Just before shooting began Jimmy entered the Palm Springs Road Races in his first Porsche, a 'Super Speedster'. He qualified for the second day's races and came second overall. According to another driver, though, he was a real danger on the track: 'He wanted to win too much and would take any kind of chance to be first.'

At the same time *East of Eden* had opened in Los Angeles and Jimmy became a national figure. The reaction of American teenagers, who at last had a star they could identify with, was way beyond Warner's expectations and fan clubs were formed all over the USA. He was mobbed in all his favourite haunts.

Like many emotionally troubled people, Jimmy found it too much; he had always wanted to be the centre of attention, but the fact that he could never escape it and that people were hanging on his every word was overwhelming, and he resumed seeing a psychoanalyst.

Giant had now begun filming in Virginia where George Stevens heard that Jimmy had entered another race. Unlike Nick Ray, who thought it was good for Jimmy to have an outlet of his own, where he could be successful on his own account, Stevens was worried about his valuable property. Consequently, he banned Jimmy from racing until filming was over. This didn't stop Jimmy ordering a Lotus IX in his search for more speed.

RACING TO DEATH

The film crew of *Giant* moved to the West, to the small town of Marfa, and Jimmy began shooting on 3 June. This was his first big-name film, as Elizabeth Taylor and Rock Hudson were also starring. Stevens and Jimmy, however, didn't get on very well — there was a conflict of wills, even though Jimmy was to admit that Stevens was getting a good performance out of him.

In August, after shooting, Jimmy took delivery of another car, a Porsche 550 'Spyder' which was significantly faster and more unstable than his Speedster. Many of his friends were disturbed by the car, which was silver and very, very low, making it difficult to see.

He left for Salinas, to race his new toy. He had asked several of his friends, and even asked his father, to accompany him on the trip, but they were all unable to. The plan had been to tow the car on a trailer, but Jimmy decided to drive it with his mechanic. On the way, Jimmy and the follow-up car with the trailer were booked for speeding. This didn't deter Jimmy as he resumed his journey, agreeing to meet his escort at Paso Robles, 150 miles up Route 466. Bill Hickman, who was in the escort car, warned him to slow down — it was early evening and the Porsche was not highly visible, but Jimmy just laughed this off.

About half an hour later the Porsche was approaching the 'Y' junction between Routes 466 and 41, a notorious blackspot. Jimmy overtook one witness at a speed of at least 85 mph, and maybe much more. A Ford saloon drew on to the highway. A collision was inevitable. The tiny Porsche smashed into the Ford and virtually demolished itself. The jaw and femur of the race mechanic, Rolf Weutherich, were broken. Jimmy had 'a broken neck, multiple broken bones and lacerations' according to the doctor's report. He had been almost decapitated, and was certified 'dead on arrival' at the Paso Robles War Memorial Hospital. So, in a way, a legend died and so, in a way, a legend was born.

▼ *On the fortieth anniversary of his death in 1995, flowers surround the grave of James Dean. Just three films had secured the actor's reputation as one of the great icons of this century's popular culture.*

Isadora Duncan

Modern dance pioneer

1878–1927

Born on 27 May 1878, in San Francisco, Isadora was the fourth child of Mary Dora and Charles Duncan, a suspected embezzler who later deserted his family. Life was hard and Isadora, her mother, brothers and sister had to survive on their mother's piano teaching.

They were a talented family and Isadora and her sister, Elizabeth, naturally gifted dancers, supplemented the family income by giving classes to local children. However, the family decided to go east to find professional work.

Despite auditioning with vast self-belief, Isadora had no luck until Charles Fair, manager of the Masonic Roof Garden, offered her a place in his vaudeville show. After three weeks as 'The California Faun' she refused to tour with the show. Luckily, Augustin Daly, one of the great theatrical managers, saw Isadora dance in Chicago and engaged her for his show in New York.

She had a small part in a pantomime called *Miss Pygmalion*. After three weeks the company went on tour, but it was a dismal failure. Back in New York, Daly offered Isadora a part as a fairy in *A Midsummer Night's Dream* and, in January 1896, she first danced professionally on a real stage.

Daly sent the company to tour England in the spring of 1897. By autumn the tour was over and Isadora returned to New York and resigned from the company in order to concentrate on her own ideas.

She wanted to dispense with scenery and elaborate costumes and return to the roots of dance. She would discard the tutu and ballet shoes, as well as the corset, and perform in bare feet and a Greek tunic.

Ethelbert Nevin, a composer, was a neighbour and Isadora began to perform to his work. He was so keen that he arranged a dual concert in the Carnegie Hall Music Room in March 1898.

> **Unique dancer, free-ranging spirit and passionate woman with a tragic destiny**

The controversial success of this show allowed the Duncans to move into the Windsor Hotel. No sooner had they set up their new home, than the whole hotel burned down, destroying most of their possessions. Isadora was convinced that it was time to move to Europe for good.

The Duncans managed to get a free passage on a cattle-boat. On their arrival, they found no work and ran out of money.

Just when their spirits were at their lowest, Isadora and her brother Raymond got an introduction to a leading society lady, Mrs George Wyndham. At Mrs Wyndham's Isadora met Charles Hallé and she knew that her fortunes had changed at last.

Director of the New Gallery in Regent Street, Hallé conceived a plan for a series of performances in the space. For these 'Evenings with Isadora Duncan' he enlisted his friends to give lectures on art and culture. The first performance was held on 16 March 1900.

Raymond, restless and under-employed, went to Paris, where he settled. At the close of summer 1900, Isadora and her mother joined him in the city that was to become her permanent home.

In spring 1901 Isadora and Charles Hallé met again at the Exposition Universelle. He introduced her to a number of influential people including Madame Saint-Marceau, wife of the famous sculptor. On Fridays she held a salon at which Isadora danced, to the piano accompaniment of 26-year-old Maurice Ravel. At 23 she was achieving a certain amount of fame and financial success.

Despite being quite well known she was offered little professional work, but at the end of 1901, she was invited to tour the German-speaking countries with Loie Fuller, another pioneer of modern dance. This was a great coup for Isadora, and led to her meeting the Hungarian impresario

Alexander Gross in Vienna. He offered her a 30-night run at the Urania theatre in Budapest, which she accepted at once

PLANS AND PASSION

After successfully fulfilling this contract, she returned to France, convinced she could conquer Paris. She was again received without enthusiasm. Distressed, she decided to take her family to visit the country of her most cherished artistic inspiration – Greece.

After a series of cultural and artistic experiments in Greece, Isadora travelled back through Europe, stopping in Vienna, and Berlin. On 14 December 1904 Gordon Craig, the progressive English stage-designer arrived in Berlin, visited Isadora and watched her dance. They fell in love and began an impassioned and tempestuous affair which delayed her first tour of Russia. This eventually began at the end of January 1905.

Her brief experience of Russian classical ballet convinced Isadora that her style of dance was right. After a brief visit to Kiev and Moscow, she hastened back to Berlin, where she was determined to set up a school and prove her theories.

She bought a villa in Grünewald, but before the school even started, it began to run out of money. Isadora gave a matinée at the Royal Opera House in Berlin and, unannounced, led a small group of her pupils on stage to give a demonstration. The Berlin public was appalled and withdrew its support, especially when they learned of Isadora's illicit liaison. Her response was uncompromising. Lecturing at the Berlin Philharmonic Hall, she declared 'the rights of a woman to love and bear children as she pleases'. Half the audience left and the other half booed.

▶ *Isadora Duncan the pioneer of modern dance, seen here in 1927, the year of her sudden, dreadful death in the seat of her Bugatti car.*

A TERRIBLE TRAGEDY

It became impossible for her to remain in Berlin, particularly as she was now pregnant. Gordon took her to a small seaside house in Holland. On 24 September 1906, Isadora gave birth to a girl, Deirdre, and moved back to Berlin. The relationship with Craig, however, eventually collapsed in 1907, under the weight of his volatile temperament, and her numerous affairs.

After another tour of Russia, Isadora realized that her school would never succeed. She closed it and left for Paris with her 12 most promising pupils. Her visit coincided with the first season of the Ballets Russes, which outshone her. Faced with this she decided to go to London.

She performed with her pupils at the Duke of York Theatre and was then invited to dance in New York for the first time since 1899. She was a dismal failure, either ignored or booed. To recover, she went on tour where she met Walter Damrosch, conductor

▶ Vanessa Redgrave and her daughter portray the real Isadora and child in the 1967 film of the dancer's life. The tragic death of both of Isadora's children in the River Seine was the saddest event in a life lived in the pursuit of happiness.

of the New York Symphony Orchestra, who offered her a collaborative venture. With him she at last achieved some measure of popular success. After the tour she returned to Europe.

She still needed money and determined to find a millionaire; the first one to turn up was Paris Eugene Singer. He was 43 and married with five children, but within a few weeks, they left Isadora's pupils in the care of a governess and, taking Deirdre with them, sailed to Italy on his yacht.

Isadora was caught up in life as Singer's mistress. She went on a tour of the United States with Singer, but had to call a halt when it became obvious to the audience that she was pregnant.

With her career on hold and her sister running the school, Isadora set up home in a villa on the French Riviera, where she gave birth to a son, Patrick. They moved back to Paris, but Isadora soon became bored and began to have affairs. She bought a studio in Neuilly and moved in with her children.

◀ Isadora's life was celebrated in 1967 in a movie which starred Vanessa Redgrave in the title role. Since none of Isadora's performances was filmed, this is the only way a modern audience can hope to comprehend Isadora's revolutionary, self-expressive style of dance.

Isadora and Singer were eventually reconciled and everything looked rosy. Then one day, after they had all been out, Isadora returned to the rehearsal studio and Singer went for a drive. The children were driven home in the limousine. Suddenly faced with a taxi, the driver stopped the car to avoid a collision and stalled the engine. He got out to crank up the car but it rolled away from him, slid down the embankment and plunged, backwards, into the River Seine.

Deirdre and the nurse were killed. Patrick was rushed to hospital but arrived too late to be saved. Isadora, who was then 35, was inconsolable. All of Paris came to the children's funeral.

Isadora's life and art were scarred by the tragedy. She became restless, travelling to Greece and the Balkans, before settling for a while in Italy. Just then she received the only news which could lift her spirits. Singer sent a telegram to say he would fulfil her long-cherished dream – he would buy her a school on the outskirts of Paris. She telegraphed Elizabeth to send all the girls back from Germany.

► *Isadora and the treasured protégés of her dance school. Though many people of the time were scandalized by her personal life, Isadora refused to let bourgeois opinions destroy her dream of a school for a new generation of dancers.*

Her six remaining pupils were reunited with her in France in January 1914. However, the outbreak of World War I in August destroyed her plans. At her lowest emotional ebb, she attempted to drown herself by walking into the sea, but was saved and sent away to the United States.

There she gave her first performance since the death of her children and was a huge success. But the Americans still did not think her a suitable person to start a school. Disgusted with her fellow citizens' lack of faith she left the country to go to neutral Switzerland. She left the girls there and began a tour of South America, from which she returned penniless. In September 1916, Isadora arrived back in New York, soon to be followed by her girls, whose fares had been paid by Singer. It was a temporary reconciliation, though, and in February 1917 the rift became final.

POST-WAR YEARS

Isadora's later years were marked by a string of lovers, a descent into alcoholism and problems with overeating. The war ended in November 1918 while she was in the South of France. She still cherished hopes of founding a school but of the six girls, only one devoted soul, called Irma, remained with her. In 1921, Irma loyally determined to accompany her mentor to a terrifying new Russia.

Isadora and her party arrived in Moscow on 24 July 1921 and quickly got into the revolutionary spirit. By November she had settled in and the government asked her to perform at the Bolshoi to celebrate the fourth anniversary of the Russian Revolution on 7 November. A few days later she met the man who was to make the

greatest impression on her Russian years – Sergei Essenin, an unpublished poet.

BROKEN DREAMS

On 12 April 1922, Isadora received news of her mother's death. Her immediate response was to fly to France and then to America, taking Essenin with her. But leaving the Soviet Union to enter the United States was no easy matter. She decided to facilitate matters by breaking the most sacred vow of her life – never to marry. She would wed Essenin, and on 2 May 1922 the ceremony was performed.

The couple went to Paris and, in October, to New York. American anti-Soviet feeling was on the rise and Isadora had to promise not to make political statements. The publicity meant that her few performances were all sold out, but her insistence on making inflammatory speeches before each dance caused enormous trouble.

The couple were forced to return to Paris, penniless and in disgrace. On 5 August 1923, after almost a year abroad, they returned to Moscow. The end of the relationship was only months away. On New Year's Eve, Isadora sat with the party of relative strangers, looking old and

crushed. 'I do not want to leave,' she said. 'I have no place to go. I have nobody. I am all alone.' She threw herself into what remained of her work, touring the Ukrainian towns performing to folk-songs and revolutionary marches.

Isadora's next move was to Nice where she hired a building on the Promenade des Anglais which she named the Studio d'Isadora Duncan and to which she retired to write her long-promised memoirs – an action primarily dictated by her perennial desperate need for money.

On 12 September 1927, she went out for a drive in her stylish new Bugatti. It was a rather chilly evening and the driver suggested to Isadora that she should wrap herself in a cape to keep warm.

Isadora settled her shawl around her neck and her shoulders unaware that the heavy fringe had fallen into the spokes of the wheel, which had no mudguards. As the driver revved up the engine, the first revolution of the rear wheels broke her neck. Death was instantaneous. She was buried in Paris on 19 September at Père Lachaise cemetery, beside her mother and her two beloved children.

Marvin Gaye

King of Tamla Motown

1939–1984

Marvin Pentz Gay Jnr was born on 2 April 1939, and grew up in a poor district of Washington DC. His strict religious upbringing made life hard. Dancing, movies and television were banned, and the Sabbath marked a weekly isolation from the outside world.

By 1946, six-year-old Marvin had two siblings: Frankie, aged three, and Zeola ('Sweetsie'), still just a baby. The house was a full and fearful one. Marvin Gay Snr, ruled with a Bible in one hand and a leather belt in the other.

Marvin had decided on a musical career and dropped out of school at 17. His father ordered him to get a job or to join the Services. He joined the Air Force, but was honourably discharged within a year.

His return home renewed tension between Marvin and his father, and to stay out of the way, he joined the Marquees, a local band. A step forward came with meeting Harvey Fuqua, writer and lead singer with a doo-wop group, the Moonglows. He invited them to join him, and in 1959 Marvin moved with the group to Chicago. Marvin's looks and voice were becoming a knockout combination. Fuqua recognized this, and easily persuaded Marvin to break up the band and move to Detroit.

Fuqua's interests included a record label, Anna, run by Gwen and Anna Gordy, and he and Marvin signed to it. Fuqua also formed two companies, Harvey and Tri-Phi, for which Marvin did session work.

His musical life took a promising turn when Fuqua, Tri-Phi and the Gordy sisters merged with another Detroit record company run by the girls' brother Berry Gordy, and called Tamla Motown.

Marvin's first try at finding a place on the Motown roster was an album consisting almost entirely of covers. His first single was a co-composition with Berry Gordy, 'Let Your Conscience Be Your Guide'.

Shot dead before his mother's eyes by his own father with the gun that he had given him

The credits on 'Let Your Conscience' showed Marvin's altered surname for the first time – from Gay to Gaye.

He continued writing and reward finally came with 'Stubborn Kind of Fellow', an R&B hit that gave him his place on the bus for the Motown Revue with some of the greatest names of soul music. With his marriage to Anna Gordy in 1963, Marvin Gaye seemed to have arrived.

By the end of the year Berry Gordy's time was much taken up with the Supremes, and Marvin felt his absence. Having shown that he could carry a song into the charts, he felt that he deserved more artistic freedom. He had already begun a habit of dropping out of live engagements.

He had found other ways to spend his time. His new riches and love of sport led him to help finance a football team and to back a boxer. He developed a fondness for cocaine, believing it inspired him; it would soon become a habit, then a dependency.

Despite more solo success, Marvin was still looking for his first number 1 record. Berry Gordy suggested a partner, 21-year-old Tammi Terrell. Their first single together, showed that they had something special. 'Ain't No Mountain High Enough' was the beginning of a two-year, three-album collaboration. However, in the summer of 1967, Tammi collapsed on stage with what was later diagnosed as a brain tumour.

She came to the studio in a wheelchair to record their second album, *You're All I Need*, released halfway through 1968. Marvin's

▶ *Marvin Gaye during the first years of his success with Tamla Motown. As a soul singer he had few peers, and as a songwriter he created some of the standards of the soul repertoire. His life, though, was mostly a shambles of drug abuse and destructive relationships.*

◀ Caught between his strict religious upbringing and the excesses of his adult life, Marvin Gaye revealed a tragic quality which was evident in much of his music.

solo work at this time was prolific, but he was deeply upset by Tammi's illness. He even threatened to shoot himself.

Art can come out of despair and so it was for Marvin. Producer Norman Whitfield got him to record 'I Heard It Through The Grapevine', which shot to the top in December 1968. The third Gaye/Terrell album, *Easy*, was released near the end of 1969. Terrell's illness beat her in early 1970, and Marvin, who had watched her fight and lose, was grief-stricken.

FINDING NEW HOPE

After Tammi's death, he was reluctant to visit the studio and he didn't perform for a couple of years. It was rumoured he had retired from Motown, who didn't know what he was up to. Their move to Los Angeles didn't help.

The Vietnam War was politicizing music. Marvin responded with the successful anti-war song 'What's Going On' and released an album with the same title.

For a while, Marvin enjoyed the wave of success. In demand, he agreed to some public appearances, but broke all but one. After producing such a classic album, he felt he deserved a break.

By now Marvin had followed Motown to Los Angeles, where in 1973 he met 16-year-old Janis Hunter. He was immediately struck by her, and his music was given an emotional boost by his passion for her.

His next album was *Let's Get It On*, released in late 1970. The title track was a number 1 single, selling more copies than 'I Heard It Through The Grapevine'. With a new contract and a hit album, Marvin could choose any direction. To many people's surprise, he rented a secluded cabin in the hills with Janis Hunter. He felt as though he was living in heaven, away from the prying eyes of the world, the pressures of business and the anger of his wife.

He came out of retreat in the summer of 1974, moving to Hollywood. In August he set off on tour, partly for the guaranteed receipts, but also to silence those who said he couldn't do it. The tour was a sell-out but the strain and the drugs took their toll.

Janis was pregnant and he was desperate to get back to her. A daughter, Noon, was born in September. Marvin immersed himself in his new family, and so began another period without a new release. By 1975, however, he had received notice that Anna was beginning divorce proceedings.

Like everything he didn't want to think about, he ignored the divorce. Janis was pregnant again, and they moved to a ranch in the San Fernando valley. His moods were changeable, and he started to lose control of the relationship. The birth of a son, Frankie ('Bubby'), in November 1975 gave the 36-year-old Marvin another period of familial calm.

DRUGS AND DESPAIR

He was persuaded back into the studio by Berry Gordy. The resulting album, *I Want You*, was released in March 1976. As the year continued, Marvin began to run out of money. He went on a European tour, but his earnings were insufficient. The following March the divorce came through, and Marvin was forced back to the studio. The financial settlement had been an imaginative coup from Marvin's lawyer. Anna would receive the $305,000 advance from Marvin's next album, plus another $295,000 of its royalties.

He considered making a quick, worthless album to get the debt out of the way, and then decided to go to the other extreme. *Here, My Dear*, a double album, chronicled the story of the marriage. It was finally released in December 1978.

By this time Marvin had been married to Janis for 14 months, but his jealousy and promiscuous lifestyle were putting pressure on them both. The costs of the divorce also added to Marvin's other obligations and disasters, and he was forced to file for voluntary bankruptcy in mid-1978.

With the urgent need for cash, Marvin took to the road, but collapsed from physical exhaustion coupled with drug over-use. Meanwhile, Janis had taken the children with her to her mother's house.

A new album, *Love Man*, was rejected by Motown and then Janis ran off with another man. Marvin toured Hawaii and Japan, returning to Hawaii in late 1979, where he met Janis and the children. They just fought, so she returned to her mother. By April 1980, he was living in a converted bread van, penniless, and suffering from cocaine-induced impotence.

In his despair he started reworking the *Love Man* tracks. He was persuaded to to do a postponed European tour and flew to London in June. Drugs and women thrust themselves at him and he started ducking engagements. The idea of returning to America, tax problems and the threat of divorce from Janis made London seem more attractive, so Marvin stayed on.

His next album, *In Our Lifetime*, brought out in January 1981, was not a commercial success. Marvin claimed that the tapes had been smuggled back to America before they were finished. He was so angry that he dissociated himself from the album and refused to work with Motown again.

Marvin returned to depression, drugs and disorder. He was rescued by Belgian promoter and fan, Freddy Cousaert, who took him off to Ostend. The animosity

◄ *After years of battling with drug problems, money problems, and wife problems, Marvin Gaye returned to live with his mother and father in August 1983. It was to be a move which a few months later sealed his fate.*

against Motown lasted, and in April he left the company after 20 years. Nearly a year later he signed a deal with CBS Records.

A FATAL RETURN

He was working on new material in June 1982 when he was reunited with Fuqua. Marvin invited him to Belgium and Fuqua brought order to Marvin's tortuous recording process. When the tapes were delivered to CBS in September, they exceeded all expectations. 'Sexual Healing' was the strongest song and the first single from *Midnight Love*, both released in November. Marvin returned to America to promote the album. Grammy awards in 1983 for Best Instrumental Performance and Best Male Vocal belatedly acknowledged an artist with 26 albums and 40 hits.

Marvin returned to his parent's house partly because his mother was undergoing

surgery; his father had moved back to Washington, so he could be with her during her recuperation.

He was in need of money again, and made an American tour in 1983. His drug intake always rose on the road and his mental stability suffered. On 1 April, Marvin's father, unable to find a document, went upstairs and ranted at his wife. Marvin hit him, pushing him on to the landing. Marvin Snr went to his room, returned with a .38 revolver and shot his son twice.

A half-hour delay followed the arrival of the ambulance because the paramedics would not go in until the gun had been recovered. Earlier help might have stopped the massive blood loss that killed Marvin Gaye – the day before his 45th birthday.

Three days later, ten thousand people filed past the open coffin for a last glimpse of a legend. His ashes were scattered at sea.

▼ *The last family row between Marvin and his father took place on 1 April. It quickly degenerated into violence, and in a drunken rage his father shot him in the back. His funeral was a massive outpouring of grief at the enormous loss to the world of music.*

Jimi Hendrix

Wild man of rock

1942–1970

On 27 November 1942, Al Hendrix was in the US Army, not in Seattle with his young wife, Lucille, when she gave birth to a son. When Al did return three years later, the boy, named John Allen Hendrix, had been fostered out. Al took John back and, on 11 September 1946, renamed him James Marshall Hendrix. A quiet boy, James had an uneventful childhood. His passion from an early age was music, and the guitar quickly became his favourite instrument.

His first gigs were as a member of a covers band while in high school. He dropped out at 17 and joined the army, taking his guitar with him. He broke his ankle during a parachute jump and was honourably discharged before the Vietnam War got started. He formed a band in the army and after his discharge he moved to New York.

Shortly after, The Isley Brothers arrived in town, needing a guitarist – Hendrix was given an audition and the job. This was followed by backing work with B B King and Sam Cooke, until in late 1965 he joined Curtis Knight and The Squires.

With Curtis Knight, he gained his first songwriting credits, and had more access to studios. During one gig he was noticed by Linda Keith, girlfriend to Keith Richards. With her financial help Hendrix gathered a band together which he called Jimmy James and The Blue Flames.

In July 1966, an introduction to The Animals' bassist and would-be producer Chas Chandler set Hendrix on to the fast lane. After one hearing, Chandler offered Hendrix a trip to London, and secured the guitarist a cash advance. On 24 September 1966, Hendrix left New York.

Chandler took him immediately to a three-hour jam with a much impressed blues player, Zoot Money. A week later, on 1 October, Hendrix was invited to play with Cream at their Regent Polytechnic gig.

> **Explosive genius of the electric guitar, Hendrix was, in every way, 'experienced'**

Within the first few bars of Howlin' Wolf's 'Killin' Floor' it was obvious that Hendrix was a major new talent in town.

Chandler set about auditioning a band for Hendrix. Ex-Loving Kind guitarist Noel Redding took the bass, while Mitch Mitchell came in on drums. The band was finalized just in time, for Hendrix's jam at Blaise's club caught the attention of French star Johnny Hallyday, who invited him to back him on a tour of France in ten days time. With minimal rehearsing, a name change to Jimi, and the decision to call the band The Jimi Hendrix Experience, they played their French dates to wild acclaim.

Back in England, the band played several showcase gigs at clubs which drew the music industry's key players: Hendrix was being tested at the highest level. Between gigs and rehearsals, the band recorded 'Hey Joe', the song which had first struck Chandler. It was Jimi's first vocal recording, and Chandler's first production job. It was backed with Hendrix's first original composition, 'Stone Free'.

The Experience got themselves a record contract with Track Records. The deal was struck at their first meeting, and 'Hey Joe' was released on Polydor on 16 December 1966. Hendrix's underground exposure and an appearance on television helped the record into the charts at number 38, peaking at number 4. Hendrix had been unleashed, and followed this single with 'Purple Haze/51st Anniversary'. More gigs followed, and by the end of January 1967 Hendrix had won over London's musical elite. It had taken just four months.

▶ *Jimi Hendrix, with Mitch Mitchell (left) and Noel Redding (right) played together from 1966-69 as The Jimi Hendrix Experience. Created by Hendrix's manager Chas Chandler, the band became a showcase for the guitarist's superlative talent.*

Jimi as a child – with his father Al. The boy was originally named John, but it was his father who renamed him James after his return from the war.

Chandler had already talked business with the Animals' manager, Mike Jeffery. While The Experience were touring and recording 'The Wind Cries Mary', Jeffery took over their management.

Released on 27 March 1967, 'Purple Haze' entered the charts at number 37. Meanwhile, Chandler had got the group a place on the Walker Brothers tour. At the Astoria gig, Hendrix set his guitar alight, causing a sensation. The publicity helped the second single climb to 3 in the charts.

A TRIUMPHANT EXPERIENCE

Sessions for the first album continued. Songs like 'Foxey Lady' and '3rd Stone from the Sun' had appeared like magic out of previous sessions. After 'The Wind Cries Mary/Highway Chile' was released in Britain, and 'Hey Joe' in America, the album *Are You Experienced?* was brought out on 14 May and leapt to number 3 in the album charts. At the beginning of June, with the help of a good word from Hendrix fan Paul McCartney, The Experience were booked for the Monterey Festival on 18 June.

The performance gained The Experience a run of dates with Jefferson Airplane and Big Brother and The Holding Company at the Fillmore West, together with an unannounced free show in Golden Gate Park in San Francisco. They played and partied their way into the hearts of the city. During this visit Hendrix was introduced to the dangerous pleasures of LSD.

The band returned to London at the end of August 1967, to see 'The Burning of the Midnight Lamp' charting at number 29. Work was begun on material for a second album. Hendrix's reputation made organizing sessions more difficult, with the number of musicians who wanted to play on sessions and with huge numbers of hangers-on ready to party.

Most of the new work was more complicated; Hendrix was keen to make the records different from the live sound. The track 'Bold as Love' featured an early phasing technique with which he was so pleased that the finished album *Axis: Bold as Love* would be named after the song.

What would prove to be The Experience's last British tour got them through November and early December, as *Axis: Bold as Love* entered the album charts at number 8. More studio work laid the foundations for the next album, but also

exposed the cracks between Hendrix and Chandler. Marijuana and speed had regularly been a part of Hendrix's socializing, but the disruptive power of LSD finally came between the two friends.

On a Swedish tour in January 1968 Hendrix was arrested after a hotel fight. He was allowed to play the concerts and escaped imprisonment only through Chandler's help. On Jeffery's insistence, the band flew to New York, chosen as their new base, to begin a lengthy tour.

The Experience roared into San Francisco on a bill with Albert King and John Mayall's Bluesbreakers, and set off around the country. After the tour, in April, Hendrix got down to work on the next album, but the tensions among the band were palpable, and matters were not helped by Jeffery supplying Hendrix with drugs. Chandler decided to abandon any more production work for the band, but continued on the managerial side. He would eventually give up even this role, after disagreements with Jeffery.

▶ *Jimi with the instrument he made completely his own. Being left-handed, he was forced to play his guitars upside down, not that this made any difference at all to his superlative talent and amazing musical imagination.*

BREAKING UP

Daytime sessions were for serious work, while the nights were used for jamming. Work on the album continued. Experimentation allowed for lots of musical combinations to be tried out, and the most successful ones found their way on to *Electric Ladyland*.

Electric Ladyland was released in October 1968. Although it was critically acclaimed, Hendrix was dissatisfied with the finished product, and had been totally unprepared for the picture of 19 naked women on the British Track Records cover. The album entered the American charts at number 31 on its way to number 1, with *Are You Experienced?* still in the Top Ten.

Despite their popularity, The Experience were becoming more fragmented and were beginning to separate, Redding with his band Fat Mattress, Mitchell with Mind Octopus, and Hendrix jamming with a wide variety of musicians. Just after Hendrix's 26th birthday party, Redding and Mitchell returned to London.

At the same time, Hendrix was producing as well as working on new songs, and enjoying clubs and parties. A record company lawyer recalled delivering some papers to Jimi and finding five girls outside the hotel suite, another answering the door and one in the bedroom with the star.

The Experience re-formed for an American tour in April 1969. In between dates there were rehearsals for the fourth album, but there was no real progress beyond the demo stage. At one point Hendrix declared he was not going on with the tour, and was still in New York at 5 pm with a gig to play that night in Detroit. He was persuaded to do the gig, but more problems followed. The next day, he was detained at customs in Toronto when heroin was found in his baggage. He was bailed and allowed to play the concert.

On 19 June 1969, Hendrix appeared at a court hearing where his trial was fixed for 8 December. He then left for California to headline at the Newport Pop Festival. This

▶ *Hendrix did undreamed of things with an electric guitar. His ability to play with electronic feedback was inspirational, and the way he played the instrument with his teeth and even set it on fire could stop any live show.*

was followed by the Denver Festival where the band encountered crowd trouble and police tear gas. Straight afterwards Redding announced his departure from The Experience.

Jeffery saw Hendrix's need for a break, and rented him a house in Shokan, 12 miles from Woodstock. There were plenty of jam sessions, which soon turned into serious rehearsals when Hendrix was announced as the headline act for the Woodstock festival. Arriving at the site on Sunday, Henrix and his band, Gypsys Suns and Rainbows, were scheduled to play next morning. From a set of mixed quality, 'Star-Spangled Banner' and 'Purple Haze' remain as a monument to Hendrix's talent at the peak of his career.

THE DANGEROUS DRUGS ACT

Hendrix left for the Toronto trial. Admitting to a list of substances he had taken and his up-front approach won him an acquittal. Delighted he returned to New York where four New Year concerts at the Fillmore East brought an ecstatic reception for his new band The Band of Gypsys. They were next due to play an anti-war benefit at Madison Square Gardens, but this was a disaster, with Hendrix completely stoned.

More American dates were planned to coincide with the April 1970 release of *The Band of Gypsys* album. The band was finding its feet live, and capacity crowds were appreciative of the new numbers like 'Hey Baby' and 'Freedom'.

Hendrix was back in the studio in August, trying to finish more tracks before a European tour that he was very unhappy

about. His leave-taking was the last time his friends in America would see him.

Hendrix was booked to play several festivals around Europe, including the Isle of Wight show. On his return to London, he declared his dissatisfaction with Jeffery, and enquired about the possibilities of breaking with his manager. He asked Chas Chandler to come back to work with him.

He spent most of the 17 September with girlfriend Monika Dannemann. In the early hours of 18 September he took some sleeping pills and at 11 am she noticed that he had been sick. His breathing was normal, but she could not wake him. She called an ambulance. By the time he got to the hospital, the mixture of alcohol and sleeping tablets had killed him.

Hendrix was buried in Seattle on 1 October 1970. He left behind him a mountain of half-finished work, a musical legacy which has made him one of the giants of the modern age.

Buddy Holly

Rock 'n' roll pioneer

1936–1959

Charles Hardin Holley was born on 7 September 1936, in Lubbock, Texas. (The more familiar 'Holly' spelling is the result of a mistake on Buddy's first recording contract.) The youngest of Lawrence and Ella Holley's four children, he was raised in the strict moral atmosphere of the Bible belt of south-west America. Music was an important part of family life, at church and at home, and Buddy, surrounded by its influence from a very early age, soon found an affinity with the acoustic guitar.

In 1949, Buddy and his friend Bob Montgomery started to play together, mostly the traditional country music of the region. By 1953 the duo was playing at every available opportunity, with a regular spot on a local radio station with their self-styled 'Western and Bop'. The same year the duo got together with a contemporary, Larry Welborn, who played bass.

For two years the band played small local gigs, until in October 1955 they got a break, kicking off two Lubbock gigs headlined by Bill Haley and The Comets and the up-and-coming 'Hillbilly Cat' – Elvis Presley. The Trio, soon joined by drummer Jerry Allison, caught the eye of Eddie Crandell, Bill Haley's booking agent, who approached several record companies on their behalf. Decca offered them a trial but Larry and Jerry, who were 17 (Buddy and Bob were 19), could not get time off school for the trip to Nashville, so Buddy took bassist Don Guess and guitarist Sonny Curtis. Decca wanted only

one vocalist for the group, and Bob persuaded Buddy to take on the role. The band recorded four tracks on 26 January 1956. Their first single 'Blue Days–Black Nights/Love Me' was released in April.

The band continued playing, and now called themselves Buddy Holly and The Three Tunes. They played exclusively rock 'n' roll, with Buddy beginning to use one of the new Fender Stratocaster guitars – the

> ## The music didn't die the day that 23-year-old Buddy Holly's plane crashed

instrument that was soon to become one of his trademarks. Another Decca session six months later produced five more tracks, including a version of 'That'll Be The Day'. The resulting single, 'Modern Don Juan/You Are My One Desire' brought as little success as the first release. A third visit to Nashville didn't impress Decca either, so early in 1957 Buddy was looking for another deal. He was, however, confident that he was heading in the right direction.

On 25 February 1957, Buddy recalled Larry Welborn and added guitarist Niki Sullivan in a trip to the nearest recording studio in Clovis, New Mexico which had been set up by musician Norman Petty. Buddy recorded the single 'That'll Be The Day' and 'I'm Looking For Someone To Love', although there was a problem with the former in that Decca still had rights over it. Because of this, they decided to hide Buddy's name under the cover of a new band; the consequent search through an encyclopedia provided the name that brought fame, The Crickets.

As well as recording them, Petty also got involved in the band's management and was soon in contact with Coral Records, which was keen enough on the band's songs to release the new single on 27 May 1957. During this time, Larry Welborn was replaced on the bass by Joe B Mauldin. Progress was not swift for the single, but it was sure and it made number 1 by the end of September.

The 21-year-old Holly's songwriting was by now as prolific as it was innovative. The industry habit of releasing only four singles a year by any one group gave Petty the idea of releasing Buddy's material on a solo basis as well as with The Crickets. So, while Brunswick Records took over the

▶ *Buddy Holly, the boy from Texas who revolutionized rock 'n' roll, and who left the world a sadder and poorer place for his passing.*

band releases, Coral concentrated on Buddy Holly records, bringing out 'Words Of Love' in mid-1957. Like most of his songs, it was written as a whole – words and music coming to Buddy at the same time. He didn't need to wait for the right lyric to fit a tune; the 'package' suggested itself for him to present to the band.

TOURS AND THE TOP TEN

That'll Be The Day' brought immediate star-status to The Crickets and they were booked on a four-month tour with the 'Biggest Show of Stars of '57'. The 15-minute sets by each artist provided a procession of current hits for the crowds during two exhausting shows each night.

Before the tour began, The Crickets laid down a few tracks to allow for new releases while they were away. Of the 13 tracks recorded, eight were Buddy's solo effort, including 'Everyday' and 'Peggy Sue'. In a single year Buddy had succeeded in recording some of the most influential songs in the history of rock music.

On a break during the tour, The Crickets recorded the final songs for their debut album. By its release in November 1957, both 'Peggy Sue' and 'Oh Boy!' were in the Top Ten in America. By 1 December, the band had discarded T-shirts and jeans for suits, bringing style to their image, as they appeared on the Ed Sullivan Show. About this time Buddy started wearing his famous black-rimmed glasses.

After the tour, Niki Sullivan left the band and Buddy decided to continue as a three-piece including himself, Jerry Allison and Joe Mauldin. This line-up took its place on another large bill, playing a dozen gigs over Christmas at the Paramount Theatre in New York. There were up to six shows a day, but the lack of travelling made a big difference to their energy levels. Buddy's stage persona was different from the mild-mannered man he was in private. The Paramount concerts typified his audience-rousing performing style.

After a short break, 1958 got under way with a three-week tour and a visit to a full-size studio to finish recording the Buddy Holly solo album. Of the tracks completed, only 'Rave On' was considered good enough for release. The band left the studio to get ready for a world tour starting in February.

Their first stop was Australia, then it was back to Florida. Then they were off for their only visit to Britain, where

◄ An image that is now indelibly etched into the history of rock music: the dark-rimmed glasses and Fender guitar. Buddy Holly was one of the great pioneers of rock who would not live to see the music's full flowering in the sixties.

excited fans were giving The Crickets better chart placings than those in America.

After Britain, The Crickets leapt straight into another American tour, coinciding with the release of the Buddy Holly album. Neither Buddy Holly's nor The 'Chirping' Crickets' albums were to make the charts during Buddy's lifetime, however.

Two events in June 1958, on different trips to New York, encouraged Buddy to change the organization of his career. Firstly, he recorded two songs at the Pythian Temple Studio without The Crickets and Norman Petty; secondly, he met Maria Elena Santiago. On 15 August Buddy and Maria were married in Lubbock.

GOING SOLO

Buddy's desire to work more for himself found him back at the Pythian Temple Studio in October, standing at the head of an orchestra. He had noticed a tendency towards softer rock 'n' roll in the charts, and wanted to try something along those lines. In this session Buddy laid down 'True Love Ways', and 'It Doesn't Matter Anymore'. We will never know whether he would have continued this sophisticated approach; what is sure is that he added a new slant to the possibilities of rock in what was to be his last studio session.

After this studio work, Buddy rejoined The Crickets for further touring. He then decided that it was time to make the final break with Norman Petty, something which his recent stabs at independence had been leading up to. He and Maria also wanted to move to New York.

Petty had been vital in the development of the Buddy Holly sound, but now Buddy had shown that he could work successfully with another producer as well as having his own production credits. He decided to leave, offering The Crickets the choice of moving to New York with him, or staying with Petty and the Clovis studio. He also agreed that they should keep the Cricket name – a generous gift as The Crickets

◄ *Though Buddy died when he was only 23 years old, the sheer quality of his songs ensure that, to this day, his work is remembered and emulated around the world.*

had more success than the solo Buddy Holly. Only the new guitarist Tommy Allsup was to take Buddy up on the move.

In the final months of 1958, Buddy acclimatized himself to his new life, setting up home with Maria. He did a little producing for his record company, and came up with the songs 'Peggy Sue Got Married' and 'Stay Close To Me'.

By the New Year Buddy was running short of money. Norman Petty had been responsible for all The Crickets' financial dealings. Breaking up with him without first sorting out the situation, had left Buddy in a financial stranglehold. Petty, legitimately, refused to let Buddy withdraw any money until their relationship had been officially wound up. Also, Maria was pregnant so that Buddy had to make some money quickly. The obvious way was to go back on the road. Of several possible tours, he chose the 'Winter Dance Party' which would set off at the end of January.

Despite having given The Crickets' name to Allison and Mauldin, Buddy borrowed it for the band he took on the 'Winter Dance Party'. Maria's condition made it sensible for her to stay at home, and so, at the end of January 1959, The New Crickets joined the Big Bopper, Ritchie

Valens, Dion and The Belmonts and Frankie Sardo on a coach that would have to brave the snows and icy weather of the Mid-West winter.

THAT'LL BE THE DAY...

Transport problems left the party stuck in the snow. By 2 February the musicians were all tired and dirty, and Buddy decided to hire a plane to take him and new band members Tommy Allsup and Waylon Jennings, from the gig at Clear Lake, Iowa, to Moorhead, some 400 miles (644 kilometres) away. They chartered a plane from the Dwyer Flying Service. Though inexperienced, the pilot Roger Peterson was willing to fly to Moorhead's nearest airport in Fargo, North Dakota. Learning of the plan, Ritchie Valens and the Big Bopper persuaded Allsup and Jennings to give up their places.

That evening's concert went well in front of an audience of 1,100. Afterwards Buddy spoke to Maria on the phone, telling her that he was

► *'The day the music died': newspaper headlines describe the tragic story of a plane journey which should never have been made.*

travelling ahead of the group. Early on the morning of 3 February, 1959, the four-seater Beechcraft Bonanza took off from the airport at Mason City. Minutes later it crashed, 10 miles (16 kilometres) away, killing all those inside.

The demolished aircraft was discovered at 9.30 am. The only imaginable reason for the crash was the appalling weather. Roger Peterson would have been flying by instruments alone, a skill in which he was not practised. News travelled within hours: Buddy's parents heard a report on the radio. So did Maria; she lost the baby soon after. His body couldn't be transported for another day, and the funeral took place on 7 February at the Baptist Church in Lubbock. Over a thousand people were present to stand over the guitar-engraved headstone, and messages came from all over the world, including one from Elvis Presley from his army unit in Germany.

Although that tragic morning took the life of Buddy Holly, the music lives on. News about him always finds its way into the media, including a poignant reminder, in February 1980. The police files at Mason City were being cleaned up, and the contents of one included a watch that had belonged to the Big Bopper and an unmistakable pair of black-rimmed glasses.

Martin Luther King

Civil-rights martyr

1929–1968

Martin Luther King Jnr. was born on 15 January 1929. His father, 'Daddy' King, was the pastor at the Ebenezer Baptist Church. Daddy King took his duties beyond simply serving his church, and was involved with the National Association for the Advancement of Colored People.

King first met racism at the age of six, when a white friend's father said that they could no longer play together because King was 'coloured'. His own parents explained about slavery and also made an important point: 'Don't let it make you feel you are not as good as white people.'

King's progress through school was fast. At 15 he went to Morehouse College, a theological college in Connecticut. Here, he expressed doubt about the value of religion, but was eventually convinced of its relevance to the civil-rights struggle. At 19 he was ordained. With a degree in sociology, he went to Crozer Theological Seminary in Chester, Pennsylvania, to study for a degree in divinity. He came top of his class and graduated in 1951. He went on to study for a doctorate in systematic theology at Boston University.

After completing his studies, King felt that he should return home. Accompanied by his new wife, Coretta, he began work at Dexter Avenue Baptist Church in Montgomery, Alabama. The church was attended mainly by the educated black middle class. Once installed, he set about organizing his congregation. His interest

in the community and his effective oratory made him a popular and respected figure.

Montgomery, in the Southern heartland, had strict segregation laws; for example, rules about what black passengers could and could not do on buses. Resentment at these rules ran high. On 1 December 1955, Rosa Parks refused to give up her seat to a white and was taken to jail. On 5 December the local black ministers met to

> **Human rights campaigner, King was shot before his dream could come true**

discuss organizing a boycott. King, at only 26, was elected their spokesman.

Out of this meeting came the Montgomery Improvement Association. King had 20 minutes to prepare an address to be given to about 5,000 people. His speech had two major thrusts: democracy and over-throwing oppression. He urged blacks to stand up for themselves and also appealed to their self-discipline.

The bus company and the city refused to agree to their demands, so the MIA organized a car pool, which the police harassed, arresting black drivers, including King. On 1 February the MIA's lawyer challenged the Alabama segregation laws in a federal court. At the end of February a grand jury charged the MIA's leadership with breaking a 1921 anti-boycott law. Rather than wait to be arrested, all 89 leaders presented themselves at the court-house in front of a cheering crowd.

The boycott ran for 381 days, attracting national and international interest. The Supreme Court banned segregation, serving an order on Montgomery's white officials on 20 December 1956. King received world-wide acclaim – and the approval of white liberal America.

NON-VIOLENT PROTEST

Soon after, King helped found the Southern Christian Leadership Conference, a non-violent movement aiming to banish segregation. In 1957, the SCLC turned its attention to voter registration. King believed in democratic change and that it was vital for blacks to use the right to vote. The 1957 Civil Rights Act redressed the fact that they did not have the vote in many states, but the response to the registration drive was disappointing.

Despite the SCLC's slow progress, King's world-wide reputation was growing. He deliberately kept the race issue to the fore, not clouding his message by associating

▶ *'...and when we allow freedom to ring, ...we will be able to speed up that day when all of God's children, black men and white men, Jews and Gentiles, Protestants and Catholics, will be able to join hands.'*

with other radical political movements. Nor, given the Cold War, did he wish to give his enemies any chance to accuse his movement of Communist influence.

In 1960 King became involved in the 'sit-in' movement; black students would go to cafés and such and demand service. King participated in Atlanta where he and 51 others were arrested in October. He had to appear before an ultra-bigoted white judge, who sentenced him to four months' hard labour. King was clearly being victimized. Two days later, he was granted bail after the intervention of Senator Robert Kennedy, future Attorney-General and brother of the then Presidential candidate, John Kennedy.

Once in power, the President's support for civil rights was tepid. He did not want to alienate Democrat voters in the South. Black students took the initiative, forming the Student Non-violent Coordinating Committee to try to speed up federal adoption of civil rights. They protested in some of the most reactionary parts of the South. They were beaten up, arrested,

◀ *Killing a dream is not so easy as killing a man. King's widow, Coretta, wrote* My Life with Martin Luther King Jnr *to help keep the vision alive.*

jailed and shot, but they did not give up. The Congress of Racial Equality started Freedom Rides, travelling with whites and trying to use all the facilities en route, a protest that was greeted with white mob violence. As a result of the Freedom Rides, the Interstate Commerce Commission finally outlawed segregation in 1961.

COUNTER-STRATEGIES

The next confrontation took place in the town of Albany, Georgia. Chief of Police, Laurie Pritchett, had made plans to deflate the protest. He had read King's book Stride Towards Freedom, and realized that brutal handling of the demonstrations would lead to federal intervention, a grave threat to Southern segregationists. Anticipating King's arrival and tactics, he drilled his men for months so that they would handle the demonstrators effectively without violence. The Albany movement faded out, without gaining any of its demands, and riven by dissension.

To avoid the mistakes of Albany, the SCLC inner council met to plan a campaign in

Birmingham, Alabama, a town renowned for its racism and a fertile recruiting ground for the Ku-Klux-Klan. Eugene 'Bull' Connor, its Public Safety Commissioner, was an unrelenting bigot. The SCLC hoped to provoke him into violence to discredit him. Initially he showed restraint, though King was jailed. While in solitary confinement he read an attack on the aims of the protest by white clergymen. In response he wrote the 'Letter from Birmingham City Jail'. This did much to persuade the Northern churches – over a million copies were printed – to follow their consciences and to urge demonstrations against racism.

King was tried locally, and convicted of criminal contempt. When he came out of jail, he found that the protest was receiving less support than he had hoped. James Bevel, a young activist in his team, suggested recruiting children. Thousands of black schoolchildren converged on the starting-point for the demonstration. Connor cracked, and King achieved the sort of publicity that the campaign craved.

Connor ordered his men to wade in brutally, setting dogs on demonstrators and bystanders alike, and having the fire service hose them down. Hundreds of children were arrested. This was fully reported in the world's media and seen on TV in the US and overseas. President Kennedy went on television on 11 June and declared civil rights to be a moral issue. On 19 June a new Civil Rights Bill

was submitted to Congress. King seemed to be getting the commitment he wanted from the white Government.

LET FREEDOM RING

To maintain the pressure, it was decided to hold a March for Freedom in Washington. On 28 August 1963, 250,000 demonstrators turned up in the nation's capital. By the Lincoln Memorial, King reminded his audience of Lincoln's Emancipation Proclamation and then fell back on the rhetoric of the black Baptist preacher:

'I have a dream that one day this nation will rise up and live out the true meaning of its creed, "We hold these truths to be self-evident, that all men are created equal." … I have a dream that one day on the red hills of Georgia, sons of former slaves and sons of former slaveholders will be able to sit down together at the table of brotherhood. I have a dream that one day even the state of Mississippi, a state sweltering with the heat of injustice, sweltering with the heat of oppression, will be transformed into an oasis of freedom and justice. …I have a dream that one day in Alabama, little black boys and black girls will be able to join hands with little white boys and white girls as sisters and brothers.'

The crowd responded ecstatically, but Southern whites did not easily surrender a system that favoured them. Black leaders were worried about lack of support from Northern whites. Meanwhile, as civil-rights leaders were attacked and jailed, the FBI looked on. King accused the FBI of supporting Southern segregationists, making him a marked man in the eyes of J. Edgar Hoover, the Director. Obsessed with the threat of Communism, Hoover insisted that his agents find links between King and Communism. Throughout 1963 and 1964 the FBI pursued King, and tried to prevent him receiving the honours and awards being showered on him, one of which was the Nobel Prize for Peace in 1964.

The 1964 Civil Rights Act had not enfranchised all Southern blacks and King

◄ *President Kennedy invited civil-rights campaign leaders, including King (left), to the White House following his special message to Congress on 28 February 1963.*

NOT SAFE, BUT RIGHT

King decided that his real target should be economic injustice and began the Poor People's Campaign. On 18 March 1968 he went to Memphis to support dustmen striking for union recognition and a wage rise. Ten days later, he led a protest to City Hall, which quickly degenerated into violence. King's supporters persuaded him to organize a more successful march.

On 4 April, he learnt that a federal judge had rejected the city's request that the planned march should be banned. But King never made it to the event: that evening, standing on his motel balcony, he was shot. We may never know who conspired to assassinate him – it has been suggested that the FBI was involved, as it feared his becoming a black Messiah.

In 1983, Congress recognized King's stature as a human rights' campaigner by making his birthday a national holiday, just as are those of George Washington and Abraham Lincoln.

made this his next aim. He turned his attention to Selma. The local sheriff, Jim Clark, was a typical redneck. On 7 March 1965, 600 demonstrators began a march from Selma to Montgomery. Clark's men and state troopers, mounted and on foot, assaulted them with batons, whips and tear-gas. This was seen on television and America was disgusted. President Johnson called in federal troopers to protect the marchers, showing the first Government support for the campaign. He had been considering a voting rights bill and the nation's reaction spurred him on. The bill was presented to Congress on 6 August 1965. It seemed as if the struggle was over.

Yet over half the black population of the US lived in the North, with the same rights as whites, but their economic position prevented them from enjoying these rights. Within days of the bill being signed, on 11 August 1965, a massive riot occurred in the Watts ghetto of Los Angeles.

Watts was a revelation to King. He realized that the economic problems of blacks were even greater than those of discrimination. He decided to take the non-violent protest to the North, but he alienated his white liberal support, and received minimal response from urban blacks.

The Vietnam War was absorbing the Government's attention at this time. King had not spoken out against it because it would have lost him Johnson's support, but the escalating cost of the war at the expense of the War on Poverty initiative at home destroyed King's faith in the American dream. He denounced the war outside the UN building in New York. Johnson was furious, as was most of the media. Riots broke out in Detroit and elsewhere, in which 83 people, mostly black, were killed.

► *'And there comes a time when a true follower of Jesus Christ must take a stand that's neither safe, nor politic nor popular, but he must take that stand because it is right.' King took – and died for – that stand.*

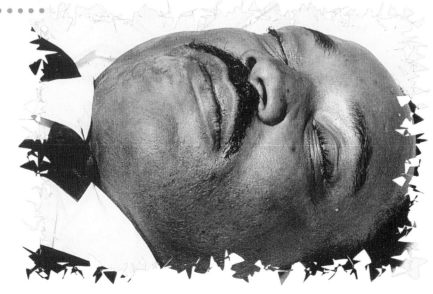

Bruce Lee

Martial arts filmstar

1940–1973

On 27 November 1940, the Year of the Dragon, Bruce Lee was born in San Francisco. His father, Lee Hoi Chuen, was a minor star of the Cantonese Opera Company of Hong Kong, then on tour in the USA.

Lee Hoi and his wife Grace named their fourth child Lee Jun Fan, which means 'return again'. Early in 1941 the family returned to Hong Kong, but within a year, war broke out. Bruce's early years were overshadowed by the Japanese occupation. With the departure of the Japanese in 1945, the people began to reconstruct the city. Entertainment was among the first revived industries and Lee Hoi Chuen was soon back in regular acting work.

Bruce became a child movie star through his father's show business connections. Aged six, he was given a role in the Hong Kong film, *The Beginning of a Boy*. A second role followed two years later. By the time he was 18, he had appeared in 20 films.

Bruce began learning kung fu in 1949. He had complained to his parents of being bullied at school and asked to be trained in the martial arts. His parents agreed to pay for him to receive lessons from Sifu Yip Man, a great master of the *wing chun* ('beautiful springtime') school of kung fu.

From 1949 to 1959, Bruce attended Yip Man's *kwoon* (training club) to learn the secrets of wing chun, growing in *chi* (inner energy) and skill. The style suited Bruce well and his devotion to the art was total.

By the age of 18, he was a kung fu expert, and had begun to form his own ideas of style. Yet he retained a respectful loyalty to Yip Man and wing chun. In early 1959, pupils of a rival kwoon challenged those of the Wing Chun School to a non-violent , sparring encounter. It soon turned ugly and Bruce was arrested. To secure his release, Mrs Lee had to sign a paper, assuming responsibility for his future conduct. A family council agreed that it

> ## Bruce Lee died just before the première of the film that brought him worldwide fame

would be wise to send him out of trouble's way – to America. So Bruce returned to San Francisco, the city of his birth.

He landed in America as Bruce Lee, US Citizen. At first he lived in Chinatown, then Ruby Chow, a Seattle restaurant owner, offered him work. Moving to Seattle, Bruce went back to school, earned his high school diploma, and in 1962 enrolled at the University of Washington.

In Seattle Bruce started teaching kung fu, to small groups of Asian martial arts fans, and later to anybody who was interested. He also constantly worked on progressing his own universal, simplified, fluid version of kung fu, which he would later term *jeet kune do* ('the way of the intercepting fist').

Bruce realized that an Eastern method of self-defence could be used to achieve the American Dream – to make money. Late in 1963, he opened the Jun Fan Gung Fu Institute at 4750 University Way in Seattle.

Not all of Bruce's mind was concentrated on his philosophical studies, kung fu and money. On 26 October 1963, he went on a date with Linda Emery, a fellow university student. They continued to see each other, and by 1964 had married and moved to Oakland California, where Bruce had set up a second branch of his Institute.

The Oakland Gung Fu Institute soon had a full roster of students, but success can attract trouble. In December 1964, the elders of San Francisco's Chinatown sent Bruce a message. They wanted him to end the lessons to non-Asians. He refused. Less than a week later, Bruce was formally

▶ *Bruce Lee, the great exponent and popularizer of the ancient art of kung fu in his last film,* Enter the Dragon. *Lee was never to see the phenomenal success of the movie, dying as he did a few weeks before its première.*

◀ *The martial arts adventure film was already an immensely popular genre in Hong Kong, but it was the great talent of Bruce Lee which took it to an international audience.*

wallet. He had been paid $400 a week during filming, now suddenly, he was forced back to a dwindling income from the kwoon, plus an occasional acting spot.

To make matters worse, in 1970 Bruce injured himself badly during a weight-lifting session. Doctors diagnosed permanent damage to his fourth sacral nerve and said he would never practise kung fu again.

Barely able to move, Bruce still refused to believe that he would be disabled, convinced instead that his will could triumph. After six months he began exercising again, and within a year seemed his old physical self. Away from the public gaze, however, he would suffer chronic pain for the rest of his life.

There was, though, one place in the world where Bruce could still be sure of work – Hong Kong. Raymond Chow, a

Hong Kong film producer, offered him US$15,000 for two Chinese martial arts features. The money put up by Chow, plus his recent rapturous reception in Hong Kong, convinced Bruce to return to the East. In July 1971, he arrived in the remote Thai village of Pak Chong for the shooting of *The Big Boss*.

Pak Chong was a humid, cockroach-infested hamlet. Fresh vegetables and meat were scarce and Bruce relied on bottle after bottle of vitamin pills to keep his body going during the six weeks of filming.

Trouble soon brewed on the set. Directors came and went, there was no proper stunt equipment and during the first week of shooting, Bruce slipped on a mattress and sprained his ankle. Then he caught 'flu. Yet, by the time of the final wrap, Bruce

▶ *Born Lee Jun Fan in the Chinese year of the Dragon, Bruce Lee began his film career as a child actor in Hong Kong. He was to return to the big screen as an adult in 1971 in the Chinese martial arts feature* The Big Boss.

challenged to a fight. Losing meant closing the institute or not teaching Caucasians. Bruce accepted immediately. One minute later the challenger had surrendered.

THE RISE TO STARDOM

The New Year of 1965 opened with both joy and pain. A son, Brandon, was born in February. A week later, Bruce's father died. Meanwhile, the Oakland Institute was not doing so well as had been hoped. Bruce began to consider abandoning kung fu as a way of earning a living.

At the end of February, as Bruce pondered his future, he received a phone call from television producer William Dozier. He wanted Bruce for 'Number One Son' in a television version of *Charlie Chan*. This idea was soon scrapped in favour of a show based on the crime-fighting comic strip, *The Green Hornet*. Bruce would play Kato, chauffeur and sidekick to the hero. He was put under option for a fee of $1,800. With Hollywood beckoning, Bruce and Linda moved to Los Angeles in March 1966.

The Green Hornet went into production in 1966, but lasted only six months, though everybody, from kids to critics, was dazzled by Bruce's kung fu. The cancellation was a blow not just to Bruce's ego, but to his

had high hopes for the film as a martial arts action movie. The première was set for early October in Hong Kong.

EAST MEETS WEST

Bruce, meanwhile, was flown back to the USA by the Hollywood studio, Paramount. An episode of the crime show *Longstreet*, 'The Way of the Intercepting Fist', guest-starring and co-written by Bruce, had just been aired to thunderous acclaim. His mind whirling with offers and counter-offers, Bruce flew to Hong Kong for the première of *The Big Boss*, accompanied by Linda and his two children. They were met at the airport by ranks of screaming fans and frantic newsmen. The première of *The Big Boss* took place at midnight. After two hours of non-stop action, the audience went wild.

Despite seductive offers, Bruce was a man of his word and fulfilled his contract with Raymond Chow. *Fist of Fury* (*The Chinese Connection* in the USA and UK), the next film for Chow, was shot in Hong Kong.

Fist of Fury smashed box-office records everywhere in South-East Asia. The critics loved Bruce's violent fighting techniques. Bruce Lee was now the hottest film property outside Hollywood.

Now a free agent, Bruce decided to form a joint production company, Concord, with Raymond Chow. This put him on equal footing with Chow rather than just being the hired actor. The problem of who would direct the next Bruce Lee film was easily solved: he would do it himself.

Now actor, producer and director, Bruce still needed the right script. Unable to find it, he decided to do this too. *The Way of the Dragon* (also known as *Return of the Dragon*) was to be solely a Bruce Lee project.

As might be expected from a directorial debut, the film had some rough edges, but audiences in Hong Kong hardly cared. *The Way of the Dragon* grossed HK$5 million, more money than any film before it. Bruce intended it to be the first of a trilogy, but almost as soon as *Way* was in the can,

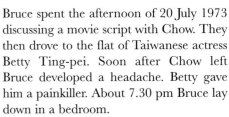

▶ *Bruce Lee was the first Chinese to become an international movie star, and his films were massive hits which were to start a trend for martial arts films which was to last for years. Sadly he was never to enjoy the fruits of his success.*

Warner Brothers made him an offer. They agreed to put up $500,000 for a martial arts movie, which would eventually reach the cinema as *Enter the Dragon*.

By February 1973, producer Fred Weintraub, director Robert Clouse and co-stars, John Saxon, Jim Kelly and Ahna Capri, had arrived in Hong Kong. None of the shoots on Bruce's films had been easy, and *Enter the Dragon* was no exception. Bruce was nervous about making his first international feature film, and delayed the start of work.

His future rode on the success or failure of *Enter the Dragon*. He worried and worked at every aspect of it, lost weight, and was living on vitamin pills and herbal drinks. He also became suspicious, less friendly, and a darkness settled around him. Only Linda received his complete trust.

FATE TAKES A HAND

Bruce's body finally broke down on the afternoon of 10 May 1973. He was dubbing the sound to the final print when he collapsed in a fit of vomiting and convulsions. He was rushed to hospital. Dr Peter Woo, a leading neurosurgeon, was called in. He administered the drug Manitol to reduce a swelling in Bruce's brain, and prepared for surgery if this did not work. It did.

A week later, Bruce was flown to Los Angeles for a complete examination. No abnormalities were found, and the collapse was put down to an excess of fluid surrounding the brain, though its cause was not known. The collapse left Bruce shaken, but did not diminish his work rate.

Bruce spent the afternoon of 20 July 1973 discussing a movie script with Chow. They then drove to the flat of Taiwanese actress Betty Ting-pei. Soon after Chow left Bruce developed a headache. Betty gave him a painkiller. About 7.30 pm Bruce lay down in a bedroom.

He was still asleep at just after 9 pm when Chow telephoned, and Betty could not wake him. Chow went to Betty's flat and called a doctor, who came immediately. At 10 o'clock an ambulance sped Bruce to the Queen Elizabeth Hospital. Doctors rushed him into an intensive care unit and tried to stimulate his heart. It was no use. Bruce Lee was already dead. He was just 32.

There were two funeral ceremonies. The first was was a traditional Buddhist service in Hong Kong. Outside the Kowloon Funeral Parlour, a crowd of 25,000 fans wept. The second, more private, ceremony was in Seattle. Bruce was buried in the city's Lake View Cemetery, in the Chinese outfit he had worn in *Enter the Dragon*. His tombstone was inscribed simply:

'BRUCE LEE. NOV. 27, 1940–JULY 20, 1973. FOUNDER OF JEET KUNE DO'.

John Lennon

The first Beatle

1940–1980

John Winston Lennon was born in Liverpool on 9 October 1940. Julia Lennon struggled to raise him while her husband Freddie was at sea. By his return in November 1944, she was pregnant by a soldier and John was with his uncle. The new baby was adopted and Julia moved in with another man.

John's unstable early life soon showed in his character: he was thrown out of infant school. His despairing father went back to sea, and he was farmed out to Julia's sister, Mimi. He suffered from dyslexia, which brought a quirky style to his later writing. His teachers were more concerned with his bad manners, theft and bullying.

At the end of 1952 John's relationship with his mother was restored. She bought his first guitar after Elvis Presley's 'Heartbreak Hotel' gave him a musical itch. Inspired by the growth of skiffle bands around the country, John formed his first band, the Quarrymen, in 1957. On 6 July they played a gig where he was introduced to James Paul McCartney. Although a year younger than John, Paul was a better guitarist, and got himself a place in the band. Paul wanted his friend, George Harrison, to join, but he was only 14 and John would not let him join for a year.

The Quarrymen were together until 1959. By then Mimi had got John into Liverpool College of Art. Paul and George were studying at the Liverpool Institute next door, and the three played and sung through lunch and break-times. John's behaviour became even less stable after his mother was run over and killed in 1958.

He had started going steady with Cynthia Powell, a fellow student. He had moved in with his friend Stuart Sutcliffe, to form a new band with Paul and George. Sutcliffe, came up with a name, the Beetles, from the film *The Wild One*. John gave it a rhythmic slant, turning 'beet' into 'beat' and the Beetles into the Beatles.

> ## John Lennon – for many the enduring symbol of the Swinging Sixties

Their break came in August 1960 when club owner, Allan Williams, got the Beatles a residency at the Club Indra in Hamburg. They returned to Hamburg in the spring of 1961 to play at the Top Ten Club. During this trip Stuart Sutcliffe fell in love with a German girl, Astrid Kircherr, and left the band. He died a little over a year later.

Back home, the Beatles now found it easy to get gigs in a basement club called the Cavern Club and became a big attraction. A version of 'My Bonnie' was in demand at the NEMS record shop, run by Brian Epstein. Intrigued, he made the first of many visits to the Cavern in October 1961. In January 1962 he became their manager, and in April 1962 the Beatles were headlining at Hamburg's Star Club.

On 1 January, the band had made a demo for Decca, but it was rejected. The tape went to George Martin at EMI, who gave them a session in June. He was dissatisfied with the drumming of Pete Best who was replaced by Richard Starkey, or Ringo Starr. Martin was wary of the band doing their own material, but Paul's 'Love Me Do', became their first single, quickly followed by John's 'Please Please Me'.

Lennon married a pregnant Cynthia on 23 August. On 8 April 1963, John Charles Julian was born. John, had little time for family life. The band recorded an album in a single night in the middle of a nationwide tour which propelled them into a headlining role on a tour in March.

'Beatlemania' was the term coined to describe the screaming young girls who lost control every time the Beatles were mentioned, and the band's appearance on the 1963 Royal Variety Show sealed the

▶ *John Lennon in the late sixties, with the rock guru look which graced the last Beatles' albums,* Abbey Road *and* Let it Be.

◀ *The Beatles in the suits and 'mop-top' hair styles of the early sixties. This look – and, of course, the remarkable music that went with it – took the world by storm and gave the language a completely new word: 'Beatlemania'.*

nation's approval. The leap of 'I Want to Hold Your Hand' to number 1 in America was unique, and in February 1964 the band left on their first US tour. By April they held the top five positions in the American singles chart.

They followed their triumph with *A Hard Day's Night*, a film probably planned merely as a vehicle for the soundtrack, but which was successful in its own right. Later in 1964, the band made a world tour which repeated the format of ecstatic crowds and constant police protection. John became a best-selling author with his books *John Lennon in His Own Write* and *A Spaniard in the Works*, and the band released *Beatles for Sale*.

LOOKING FOR ANSWERS

John had bought a mansion in Surrey, and after the rigours of touring which had continued until September 1965, he almost hibernated there. There was a void which could not be filled by his family, for his relationship with Cynthia and Julian was minimal, so he turned to the first of many alternatives, including LSD.

After the American tour of 1966 John went straight into filming Richard Lester's *How I Won the War*. He also continued his LSD journey in London. On 9 November 1966, he met artist Yoko Ono, who was in London with her husband and also her daughter. She decided that John was for her and he was infatuated.

1967 was the high point of flower power, and the Beatles' album, *Sergeant Pepper and His Lonely Hearts' Club Band*, became the monument of the era. By now Paul was the driving force of the band, and John's resentment was a feature of a general frustration within the Beatles.

With George's encouragement, they came under the influence of the Maharishi Mahesh Yogi. On 27 August 1967, they were with him when they heard of Brian Epstein's suicide. The main project that year was *The Magical Mystery Tour*, which contained John's 'I Am The Walrus'.

▶ *John and Yoko in London in the mid-seventies, before the birth of their son Sean and a self-imposed five-year exile from the public gaze.*

The Beatles broke with the Maharishi in February 1968, after which John sank back into drug-taking. Cynthia and he had been leading separate lives for years, and after she returned from a trip to Greece, he decided to make his relationship with Yoko public, which he did in June. The couple then spent a 'honeymoon' at Ringo's flat.

BEATLES BUSINESS

The 1968 album was simply called *The Beatles*, but is known as the 'White Album'. The single from it, 'Hey Jude/Revolution', was the first on Apple Records, their own label. John and Yoko brought out their album *Two Virgins*, followed on 18 October by their arrest for possessing drugs. Two weeks later Yoko miscarried. Next week John pleaded guilty at the drugs' trial and was fined £150.

At the beginning of 1969 the Beatles began work on *Let It Be*. An attempt to film them working and also Yoko's presence were disruptive. Finally, they took the gear to the flat roof of the Apple Corp's Saville Row headquarters and played a live set.

▶ *The early Beatles at the Cavern Club in 1962, a year before they hit the headlines. It was this line-up that played the now legendary Hamburg gigs. On drums is Pete Best, who the following year, would be replaced by the irrepressible Ringo Starr.*

Their differences opened into hostility over the question of management. Paul favoured music-business lawyer Lee Eastman, but John preferred Allen Klein, accountant and Rolling Stones' manager. George and Ringo sided with John, and the row ended in an open feud.

Meanwhile, in March 1969, John and Yoko got married in Gibraltar, followed by the first 'bed-in', in Amsterdam, in an advertisement for peace. Their identity as artists of controversy and promotion was described in John's song, 'The Ballad of John and Yoko'. They went to Toronto in May for another bed-in, recording 'Give Peace a Chance' in the hotel bedroom.

BREAKING UP AND MAKING UP

In September 1969, *Abbey Road* was released, and the same month John and Yoko flew to Toronto to play at a rock 'n' roll revival show. His arrival on stage with Eric Clapton, Klaus Voorman and Alan White was the debut of the Plastic Ono Band. In October Yoko had another miscarriage. John blamed drug-use, and attempted to get himself off heroin. A trip to Greece was marked by the *Wedding Album*.

In 1970 'Instant Karma' was created, recorded and released in 10 days. Just before *Let It Be* was released, Paul announced his retirement from the Beatles. At this time John embraced Arthur Janov's Primal Scream therapy. Its results show in the self-conscious honesty of songs on the John Lennon/Plastic Ono Band album of December 1970.

1971 saw the division of the Beatles' assets. Animosity between John and Paul grew, and was made public in press interviews. Paul seemed to belittle John's activities,

and he hit back ferociously, culminating in the vinyl dismembering of 'How Do You Sleep?' on the *Imagine* album of October.

John and Yoko had settled in New York. He was mixing with some left-wing radicals, attracting the attention of the US Immigration Services, who ordered his deportation after his visa expired in February 1972. Lennon began a four-year battle for a green card, and could not leave America in case he was not allowed back.

He relied on drink and drugs to deal with the pressures. An 18-month period, known as the 'Lost Weekend', began as he left for Los Angeles with his secretary, May Pang, when Yoko kicked him out. His mind cleared enough for him to produce *Walls and Bridges* in October 1974. It contained his first number 1 American single, 'Whatever Gets You Through the Night'.

By 1975, order was returning. In January the Beatles split officially, and John got back with Yoko. He had regained his optimism and creativity, working with David Bowie on his *Young Americans* album. Yoko became pregnant.

On 9 October 1975, Yoko gave birth to a son. John saw it as a miracle, and Sean Taro Ono Lennon was treated as such. As

a coda to the era, the compilation album *Shaved Fish*, released just after Sean's birth, was a résumé of John's recent music. He now immersed himself in his duties as a house-husband and proud father.

AN ERA ENDS

An ocean voyage in August 1980 gave John a new sense of himself, sparking off a fit of songwriting. He recorded over 20 songs at an impressive speed. They were included in a new album, *Double Fantasy*, released on 17 November and revealed a new maturity. Having celebrated his fortieth birthday, he was feeling ready to capitalize on his rediscovered muse with more writing. Though thin from his new health regime, he showed undeniable energy.

Everything stopped at 10.50 pm on 8 December. Mark Chapman, 25-year-old fan and born-again Christian, put four bullets into John's back as he returned from the studio. John died at the Roosevelt Hospital, shortly after arrival.

He was cremated on 10 December at the Hartsdale Crematorium. Four days later 100,000 people in Central Park observed 10 minutes silence in his memory.

Bob Marley

Reggae voice of Jamaica

1945–1981

Robert 'Nesta' Marley was born on 6 February 1945. His mother Cedella had been deserted by Norval Sinclair Marley, a 'respectable' white Jamaican, the day after their wedding. She brought up Nesta alone in Alva, near the village of Nine Miles in St Ann, the 'garden parish' of Jamaica.

They moved to the capital, Kingston, when he was 10. Restless in the country and encouraged by her boyfriend, Toddy Livingston, Cedillla had made the move. Nesta's life was eased slightly by the presence of his friend, Toddy's son, Bunny.

They settled in one of the 'government yards' – housing built after the hurricanes of 1944 and 1951 – in the rough Trench Town area. Nesta and Bunny found Trench Town tough at first. It was a time of social and political unrest. Most boys were looked on as potential hoodlums and many grew into 'rude boys' – bitter, violent teenagers who despised authority. In time, Nesta grew used to his new surroundings, and found he loved the sense of belonging.

At 14, Nesta left school. Cedella and Toddy decided he should be apprenticed to a welder. He agreed for his mother's sake, but had ambitions of his own. He had decided to be a singer. He and Bunny had been practising in the yard, with Bunny playing along on his 'guitar' – a large sardine can strung with electrical wire.

They had also started going to the 'blues dances' held at outdoor venues around Kingston, where all the new music, including ska, was played. In the mid to late 1950s the competition between the DJ's 'Sound Systems' was almost a war. Two of the leaders, Duke Reid and Sir Coxsone Dodd, emerged as clear winners in the battle, and in 1959 Sir Coxsone set up his own recording studios, recognizing the money to be made from Jamaican music. Nesta, and all the other would-be stars, spent hours there every day.

> ## Rasta superstar cruelly cut down by cancer at the peak of his popularity

By 1962, he had written a few songs, and decided to approach Dodd. When he turned up, Dodd wasn't there, but Nesta met Leslie Kong, a Chinese-Jamaican entrepreneur. Kong ordered Nesta to sing there and then. He sang one of his own songs, 'Judge Not'. Kong recorded two songs for which Nesta got £20.

Now 17, Bob, as he now preferred to be known, had decided to become a full-time singer. He had continued to write songs with Bunny, and now they'd joined forces with Peter McIntosh. The three started going along to music workshops run by musician and Rastafarian, Joe Higgs. He soon singled out Bob for special attention.

About then, the band – The Teenagers, renamed The Wailers – acquired some extra members: a vocalist and two backing singers. They practised together for weeks before approaching Higgs, who then began to coach them seriously.

They worked hard and Higgs arranged for them to audition with Coxsone Dodd one Sunday. He offered a contract at once: he would pay £20 for exclusive rights to release their records and to act as their manager. They agreed.

The Wailers were nervous, but managed to record two ska tracks. When one of these began to catch on at his Sound System, Dodd called them back for more recording. By this time their backing vocalist had dropped out, and Dodd told them they needed a lead singer.

After discussion it was decided that Bob should lead, as 'Simmer Down', their best song, was his. Dodd liked it too; powerful, raw, and rooted in the ghetto, it dealt with street crime – speaking to the rude boys in their own language. It was a smash hit, reaching number 1 in February 1964.

Coxsone Dodd now faced a dilemma: to encourage The Wailers' individual style, or follow his plan to groom a slick R&B group. Unsure, he arranged for them to compete at a talent show at the Majestic Theatre, initiating a weekly wage of £3.00 each. Trying to please as many people as possible, he got The Wailers to sing a combination of popular Motown and R&B numbers and their 'ghetto songs'. They were a huge success, and the audience loved them, though they narrowly lost the contest.

The Wailers were very busy with live shows and new records, many of which became hits. One day, taking a short cut to the recording studio, they were accosted by a pretty teenager. Rita Anderson was later to become Bob's wife.

On Christmas Day 1964, The Wailers played at the Ward Theatre in Kingston: fights broke out as fans battled to get in. Several people were knifed and controversy raged over The Wailers and the criminals among their following. By the time The Wailers' single 'Rude Boy' came out in June 1965, discontent among the poor was running higher than ever, and the hopelessness and bitterness felt by many in downtown Kingston was expressed in the song.

BEYOND THE ISLANDS

In the autumn Cedella wrote inviting Bob to America, where she had moved after the birth of Pearl, Toddy's daughter. Tired of being manipulated by Dodd, and determined to earn enough to set up his own record label, he decided to go. He insisted that he and Rita should get married before he left. They were on 10 February 1966: she was 19 and he 21, sporting a short haircut and his black stage suit for the occasion. Like his father, he left his wife the next day.

In October Bob returned to Kingston. He hadn't saved enough to be independent, but with friends' help he built a stall to sell Dodd's records, plus some on his own new label, Wail 'N' Soul 'M. He noticed that more and more ghetto youths were becoming Rastafarians. He talked to Higgs, who explained the faith. Bunny had been a Rasta for years, and in spring 1967, Peter and Bob started growing the characteristic dreadlocks and soon embraced the faith.

The Wailers were the first Jamaican band to adopt a Rasta identity: talking in patois, following a precise diet, and smoking 'herb' (marijuana). They were still recording with Coxsone, but their output slowed, and before long they were short of money. Bob and Rita moved to St Ann.

The Wailers decided to approach Bob's first producer, Leslie Kong. He produced a

▲ Bob Marley brought reggae music to a world audience, and in doing so became a superstar. All the fame in the world, though, could not save him from a fatal brain tumour.

number of songs for them, but none of the records sold well. It seemed the band had lost their grip on the charts.

At about this time, singer Lee 'Scratch' Perry brought out 'People Funny, Boy'; it was an instant hit. It had a new, slow, beat, which was picked up by The Maytals' 'Do The Reggay' in 1968 – and developing from this, reggae became the new sound.

Perry and his band The Upsetters hit the British charts the following year, causing a sensation on tour. When they returned to Jamaica, The Wailers approached them and Bob persuaded The Upsetters to break with Perry and join forces. Perry was livid, but the two met and agreed that he would be the producer of The Wailers. Their first album, *Soul Rebels*, came out in 1970, and sold well, not just in Jamaica, but to Afro Caribbeans in Britain too.

The Wailers had been working with singer Johnny Nash and his promoter Danny Sims since 1968. In 1970, Sims organized a Wailers' tour of England. They also worked with Nash on more songs, some of which were extremely successful – for Nash. Then Nash and Sims left for Florida. The Wailers were stranded, penniless in a wet, cold, alien country.

SUPERSTAR STATUS

Desperate, Bob approached Island Records, a London company set up by white Jamaican Chris Blackwell. He knew of The Wailers' 'difficult' reputation, but also recognized the only reggae band with enough talent to make an impact on mainstream pop. He decided to take them on.

In early 1973, The Wailers' debut album for Island, *Catch a Fire*, was released to rave reviews in the music press. Roots reggae fans loved it and thousands who had never heard of reggae rushed out to buy it. Blackwell arranged a tour of England and the USA. For part of the tour they were booked to support Sly and the Family Stone, but were swiftly dropped when the crowd showed they preferred The Wailers.

The tour went well: they had really started to make a name for themselves outside the Caribbean. Personally, though, it was very different: Bunny couldn't stand the cold, and Higgs flew in to take his place on the tour. Peter grew increasingly bitter. They were no longer billed as 'The Wailers', but 'Bob Marley and The Wailers'.

Later in 1973 Island released *Burnin*. The tracks were powerful, especially 'Get Up, Stand Up' and 'I Shot the Sheriff'. Suddenly Bob was in all the papers: reggae was the hippest sound around. He was hailed as a major modern poet, but on the *Burnin* tour, tensions within the band were growing. Then came the English leg of the tour, during which Bob and Peter ended up coming to blows. By 1974 the original Wailers had unofficially split up.

Bob spent much of that year in the studio, working on a new LP, *Knotty Dread*, which to his horror was released as *Natty Dread*. Tracks included 'Rebel Music' and 'Revolution', songs with lyrics that greatly disturbed the authorities in Jamaica. While Bob was touring Europe and the USA again, the Jamaican police publicly beat up Peter Tosh (formerly McIntosh), apparently to make an example of him.

Unaware of trouble at home, Bob Marley and The Wailers were making a huge impact. With Bunny and Peter gone, harmonies were now supplied by the I-Threes, a trio composed of Rita Marley, Marcia Griffiths and Judy Mowatt.

From a 1975 tour, Island released the *Live!* album, first in Europe, and then in the USA. The band had even started to get airplay on white American rock stations, and Bob was now a fully fledged star.

His success continued. In 1976 the album *Rastaman Vibration* was released and was a great success. Album after album followed, each a bestseller, and Bob found himself a living legend, repeatedly touring the world and playing to sell-out crowds.

ONE LOVE

In June 1976, Jamaica's governor-general declared a state of emergency, putting the island under martial law. It was the lead-up to an election and there had been violence. Bob was asked to do an outdoor concert, 'Smile Jamaica', on 5 December. Assured it was an apolitical concert to help keep the peace, he agreed. However, a week before the concert gunmen tried to kill him. He played the concert, then left the island, for America and Britain, where he and The Wailers cut 20 new songs during the winter of 1977. Half of these were for the explosive *Exodus* album.

Bob did not return to Jamaica until the spring of 1978. He was asked to play the 'One Love' Peace Concert, organized by

▲ *Bob Marley was to give not only great music to the world, he was also to give his native Jamaica a source of enormous national pride. His funeral would see 40,000 of his countrymen file respectfully past his coffin.*

Jamaica's two rival political parties. The concert was a measure of Bob's stature: not only did he play sensationally, but persuaded the warring political leaders to come on stage and lock hands with his. The success of that concert seemed to give Bob a new burst of energy and he threw himself into a world tour that took in America, Europe, Australia and Japan.

All was not well, though. Bob was losing weight and had begun to look ill. The problem had started some years earlier, in 1977, when he had injured a toe playing football: the toenail had been wrenched off and the wound refused to heal. A specialist who examined Bob's foot had detected cancer cells and advised him to have the toe amputated as soon as possible

▶ *'Bob Marley was a charismatic, powerful man, who nevertheless remained somehow elusive to easy interpretation. His early death from cancer came as a blow to all those who loved great music.*

to stop the cancer spreading. Bob refused. As a Rastafarian, he saw his body as a temple – and decided to let nature take its course. The toe remained, but by 1980 it had become ulcerated and very painful, though most of the band were unaware of this.

In September 1980, Bob and The Wailers set off for the 'Uprising' tour of the USA. One morning he went out jogging with Skill Cole. They were running through Central Park, when suddenly Bob collapsed. He seemed to recover after a few hours but his doctor sent him to see a neurologist. The prognosis was bad. His

collapse had been a stroke, he had a cancerous brain tumour, and maybe only two weeks left to live.

Bob was stunned, but flew to Pittsburgh and insisted on playing the following night. It was his last gig. Further tests revealed cancer of the lungs and stomach, and as his illness got worse, arguments raged over whether to keep his condition secret. Then the doctors began chemotherapy and his dreadlocks fell out. Bob was in agony.

As a last resort his family sent him to a controversial cancer specialist in Germany. He struggled on for a further six months. In the end he weighed less than six stone and could hardly even hold his guitar. Finally, on 11 May 1981, Bob died on his way back to Jamaica. He was 36.

NATIONAL HERO

Jamaica declared a national day of mourning. Bob's body was flown home and 40,000 Jamaicans filed past to pay their last respects. He had been awarded the Jamaican Order of Merit, and a banner proclaiming 'The Hon. Robert Nesta Marley OM' was proudly displayed among flags and portraits of Bob and Haile Selassie. After the funeral service, his coffin was slowly driven back to St Ann, along roads lined with mourners, to the hill where he was born.

Freddie Mercury

King of Queen

1946–1991

Freddie Mercury was born Farookh Bulsara to Persian parents on 5 September 1946. His birthplace was the island of Zanzibar, off the east coast of Africa.

When he was eight, he was sent to school in Bombay, St Peter's English boarding school just outside the city. His friends there renamed him Freddie, a name which his family also adopted. Among the talents he discovered at school were sport and music, and it wasn't long before he had formed his first band, The Hectics.

Those days in Bombay were some of his happiest: successful and fulfilled at school, and with servants to attend to his every need at home. After finishing at St Peter's he went back to his family's flat in Zanzibar, but when he was 18 he was uprooted again. In 1964, the Bulsaras fled to England from civil unrest in Zanzibar. Their new home was a semi-detached house in the drab London suburb of Feltham, a far cry from the exotic lands of Freddie's youth. But the Swinging 60s were an exciting time in Britain.

Freddie had always enjoyed art, and in 1966 he began to attend Ealing art school. He was coming under the influence of the new music scene and was intrigued by Jimi Hendrix. He had an unfocused desire to perform, but hadn't yet found the musicians with whom to form a band.

But that was soon to change. In 1968, a physics student at London University's Imperial College, Brian May, teamed up with former dentistry student, Roger Taylor, and art student, Tim Staffell, to form the group Smile. Staffell was a fellow student of Freddie's. He started taking Freddie along to Smile gigs.

In 1969 Freddie was introduced to a group called Ibex and began singing for them. They travelled up and down the country playing small pub gigs, but were going

> **Superb showman, Freddie Mercury was a victim of an outrageous and excessive lifestyle**

nowhere fast. For a while Freddie sang with a group called Sour Milk Sea, and when they broke up he set up his own band, Wreckage. That also didn't last long. However, Freddie was still hanging out with the members of Smile.

When Tim Staffell decided to quit the band, Freddie took his place. And so it was that in April 1970 the band that would be Queen came into being, the line-up being completed in 1971 when John Deacon joined on bass. 'Queen' was Freddie's idea. Brian thought it was too camp, but Freddie insisted. He also decided that he needed a new name, and became Freddie Mercury.

It took the new group a while to get going. They did the usual round of gigs in colleges, pubs and clubs. Then, in 1972, they were talent-spotted and managed to swing a deal with record industry giant EMI. The band looked like no other band of the time. Standard rock garb was jeans and T-shirts, but when Queen strutted on to the stage they did so in silk costumes, dripping with jewellery. The group's debut single, 'Keep Yourself Alive', flopped. So did their first album, *Queen*, but their second album, *Queen II*, did better.

The band's first real success came in 1974, with 'Seven Seas of Rhye'. And from then on Queen never looked back. The album *Sheer Heart Attack* and the classic single off it, 'Killer Queen', were huge hits. And then in 1975 came the phenomenon of 'Bohemian Rhapsody'.

'Bohemian Rhapsody' almost didn't make it as a single. Its weird mix of musical styles

▶ *A consummate performer and magnificent, over-the-top showman, Freddie Mercury lived his entire life on a stage. Sadly for the world, his life of excess and self-indulgence would give him the dreadful disease that was to take his life.*

▲ *Freddie Mercury and Queen. The group glammed it up in the seventies, played the stadiums in the eighties and finally took the world by storm during the Band Aid concert in 1984. There is no doubt that they would still be going strong today had it not been for the untimely death of Freddie.*

and the fact that it is so long made executives at EMI very nervous. Then DJ Kenny Everett got hold of a copy. He wasn't supposed to play it on air, but he did whenever he could, creating such demand that EMI was forced to release it. 'Bohemian Rhapsody' was later released on an album called *A Night at the Opera*, which at the time was the most expensive album ever made. After 'Rhapsody', Queen were rock royalty. The group recorded an average of one LP a year from 1973 to 1991. They began to play bigger and bigger venues, and in fact are credited with the invention of 'stadium rock'.

Freddie Mercury must take much of the credit for making Queen the band they were. He wrote many of their smash hits, including 'Bohemian Rhapsody', 'We Are the Champions' and 'Another One Bites the Dust'. But more importantly, Freddie was the focus of the band's live show. Brian

May and John Deacon were quite shy men and Roger Taylor was hidden behind his drums, so it fell to Freddie to act as the band's showman. It was a role he relished and performed with gusto and panache.

David Bowie described him as a 'star who could hold the audience in the palm of his hand'. At Queen's famous gig in Rio de Janeiro in Brazil in 1985, almost everyone in the crowd of 325,000 joined him to sing 'Love of My Life'. In Mannheim, Germany, he conducted with his short mike stand, waving it like a royal sceptre as 80,000 Germans sang a lusty version of the British National Anthem.

Freddie was famous in the rock world for his showmanship and posing. Queen was one of the highlights of the biggest concert ever – the Live Aid show in 1985. After the show Bob Geldof described Queen as the biggest band on the planet. And he pointed out that the event had been the perfect stage for Freddie.

● ● ● ● ● ● ● ● ● ● ● ● ● ● ● ● ● ● ●

▶ *Freddie loved the decadent image that came to surround him, and played up to his reputation as a master of camp excess. Unfortunately, the onset of AIDS would end the party.*

LIVING TO EXCESS

In 1980, Freddie changed his image. He had realized that he was homosexual and decided to adopt a gay 'look'. He cut his flowing black hair, grew a macho moustache, and stopped painting his fingernails.

Freddie also had a musical career independently of Queen. Perhaps the most famous example of this work was his collaboration with the Spanish opera singer Montserrat Caballé. That song became the world-famous 'Barcelona'. The single was chosen as the official theme tune for the 1992 Barcelona Olympics. Working with the diva was one of the most fulfilling experiences of Freddie's musical career. After their album had been put together Freddie said simply, 'What else is there left for me to do?'

Freddie's life off-stage was as over-the-top as it was on stage. He told one reporter: 'Excess is part of my nature. To me dullness is a disease.' His sex life was, to say the least, active. He confessed to having an enormous sex drive. 'I'll go to bed with anything,' he boasted. 'I prefer my sex without any

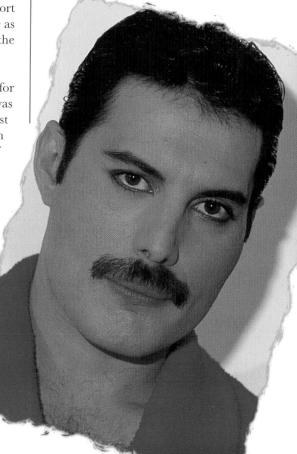

involvement. There are times when I just live for sex.'

Freddie's partying was legendary. It was routine for Queen to throw parties after their concerts, but the really extravagant bashes took place on Freddie's birthday. It was quite standard for him to splash out £50,000 on entertainments and drink. One party reputedly cost £200,000 with £30,000 spent on champagne. Drugs featured heavily, especially cocaine. Reportedly, he and his guests snorted £24,000-worth of the white powder at just one celebration.

Freddie's taste for excess extended to shopping. He once said, 'I love to spend, spend, spend.' On just one shopping trip he spent £25,000 on antiques and art. He bought a 144-piece dinner service handpainted with miniature copies of Constable paintings. Each serving plate cost £20,000. He was passionate about fine art and amassed one of the best private collections in Britain.

His Kensington home was another great and costly luxury. He bought it for cash – £500,000. It had eight bedrooms, four marble bathrooms, a jacuzzi and a minstrels' gallery. Refurbishment took years, but when it was finally ready, Freddie decided to move in for a weekend to see how it felt. He never moved out. And he brought with him his beloved cats, Oscar and Tiffany. The house would become a sanctuary for Freddie towards the end of his life, as he put his days of wild partying and high living behind him.

THE HIDDEN SIDE OF FREDDIE

Although Freddie is remembered as the camp and over-the-top frontman for Queen, there was another side to him. Inside the showman there was a troubled and lonely man. It's no surprise that one of his greatest solo hits was a cover of 'The Great Pretender'.

Many of his friends would say that his wild, gay lifestyle was only one superficial aspect of his life. His longest intimate relationship was not with a man, but a woman – Mary

Austin. She was a rock he could cling to in the storm of one-night stands and troubled relationships. They met when she was working at the 1960s boutique Biba. They lived together for seven years, and even after he began to live a gay life, Mary remained his confidante. As well as being there when Freddie needed advice or comfort, she would help the star get ready for his shows, even doing his make-up for him. In fact, many credit Mary with helping to create the showman.

Although Freddie never announced to the world that he was gay, he lived a life of promiscuous homosexuality. But he would oscillate between one-night stands and prolonged, domesticated relationships. He often said that his promiscuity was a way of hiding from his loneliness. He loved being in love and would be inspired, churning out songs and music. He could also live a very quiet life when he wanted to, tending his garden and entertaining friends at home instead of partying. Close friends say they believe he wished he could have had a family. Others say he never recovered from the shock of leaving Bombay for Feltham.

By 1986, Freddie had abandoned his life of excess. He wouldn't admit to the world that he had AIDS, but people began to suspect that something was wrong. He said he was sick of touring. 'I don't think a 42-year-old man should be running about in a leotard any more,' he declared. The truth was that Freddie knew he was dying. He no longer had the strength to strut about the stage.

His public appearances became rarer as he became a recluse in his Kensington home. When he went into the studio to record 'I'm Going Slightly Mad', it was obvious to the crew that Freddie was very ill. The technicians were told that he would tire easily, but AIDS was never mentioned. They were told that he'd hurt his knee. He had to wear thick make-up to conceal the blotches on his face and a thick T-shirt under his suit to disguise how emaciated his body had become.

SAYING 'GOODBYE'

Freddie even kept his illness secret from the other members of Queen. And it was only 24 hours before the end that he admitted to the world that he had AIDS. He released a short statement: 'I wish to confirm that I have been tested HIV-positive and have AIDS. I felt it correct to keep this information private to date in order to protect the intimacy of those around me. However, the time has now come for my friends and fans around the world to know the truth. I hope everyone will join with me, my doctors and all those worldwide in the fight against this terrible disease.'

The end came unexpectedly. His parents didn't even have time to get to his bedside before he died on the bitter evening of Sunday 24 November 1991. He was just 45 years old, proof that the candle that burns twice as bright burns half as long.

Marilyn Monroe

Lonely sex symbol

1926–1962

At 9.30 am on 1 June 1926, a girl was born in the Los Angeles General Hospital. She was registered as Norma Jeane Mortenson, but she might have been the daughter of a number of men. In two weeks her mother, Gladys Monroe, had given her to a foster family, where she stayed for the first seven years of her life. Then, Gladys reclaimed her.

That autumn Gladys became depressed over her grandfather's suicide. Her friend Grace McKee called in a neurologist, who gave Gladys drugs that divorced her from the outside world. It was Grace's turn to play mother, indulging all her motherhood fantasies and assuring Norma Jeane that she would one day be a big movie star.

Grace decided to become Norma's legal guardian. She obtained a formal statement from doctors that Gladys was insane, and bundled her off to a psychiatric hospital. Stability seemed to have arrived, but then Grace met Ervin Silliman Goddard.

They married in August, bringing one of his three daughters back to Los Angeles with them. Grace told Norma Jeane that there was no room for her. So, on 13 September 1935, she was packed off to the Los Angeles Orphans Home, where she became occupant number 3463.

Two years later Grace brought her home, but domesticity was not to last. Goddard, who had taken to drink, tried to molest Norma Jeane one night. Grace at once shipped the girl off to relatives.

From November 1937 to August 1938, Norma Jeane lived with the mother of Olive Brunings, who had married Gladys's brother. Just after her twelfth birthday, one of Olive's sons tried to assault her and, again, Grace intervened, taking the child to her aunt, Ana Lower, in Los Angeles.

In 1940 Ana developed heart problems and Norma Jeane returned to the Goddards. They had new neighbours with

> ## The secret of Marilyn Monroe's mysterious death will probably never be solved

a dashing son, Jim Dougherty. Early in 1942, Goddard was being transferred to West Virginia, and Norma Jeane was told that she was not going with the family.

On 1 June 1942 she turned 16; on the 19th, she married Jim. In spring 1944, he was called up for military service and she went to live with her mother-in-law in North Hollywood. She got a job at an aeroplane factory, and her life changed.

The Army's First Motion Picture Unit was sent to photograph women helping with the war effort. 25-year-old David Conover began taking stunning pictures of Norma Jeane and suggested she apply to the Blue Book model agency. By spring 1946 she had appeared on 33 magazine covers and was being snapped by top photographers. Her ambitions grew. She wanted to go for a screen test, but thought she couldn't work in the movies if she was married. Grace arranged a divorce.

In July 1946 Norma Jeane arrived for a screen test at Twentieth-Century Fox. She was suffering from nerves, but when the cameras rolled she was transformed. She was a natural, and a contract was drawn up. One problem remained, her name. Without hesitation she chose 'Monroe', her mother's name. Her interviewer, Ben Lyon, solved the problem of her first name; he said, 'You're Marilyn.'

Her first role was a schoolgirl in *Scudda-Hoo! Scudda-Hay!* and her only words were 'Hi, Rad!' Her contract was not renewed in August 1947. She signed a fruitless contract with Columbia, but then got lucky. She began an affair with Johnny Hyde, executive vice-president of the William Morris Agency. He got her a

► *The first issue of* Playboy *magazine featured a nude photo set of Marilyn. It was to be this kind of 'exposure' in the late-forties that led to her break into the movies in 1947.*

cameo in a Marx Brothers movie, *Love Happy*, and minor roles in *The Asphalt Jungle* and *All About Eve*. On 18 December 1950, he died of a heart attack and Marilyn promptly moved agencies to Famous Artists who, almost immediately, secured her a seven-year contract with Fox.

STARDOM – AT A PRICE

Fan mail began to pour into the studio: two to three thousand letters a week – more even than for Betty Grable or Gregory Peck. By the end of 1951 the shareholders insisted that Marilyn should star in a picture. The film chosen was *Don't Bother to Knock*, in which she played a psychopathic baby-sitter

This was followed by *Monkey Business* and a personal request to meet her from one of America's baseball legends, Joe diMaggio. They began an affair early in 1952.

In June, it was announced that she would have second billing in *Gentlemen Prefer Blondes*. On 26 June, 1953 Marilyn and the film's star, Jane Russell, placed their hands and feet in wet

◀ It was during her years in modelling that Marilyn first learned how to act to camera, and in the years after 1947 she perfected her skill, until by the mid-fifties she was the most photographed and filmed woman in America. That is when her problems really started and she never found the security and love she craved.

cement outside the Chinese Theater on Hollywood Boulevard, and Marilyn knew that at last she had arrived.

On 14 January 1954, she flew to San Francisco to marry Joe diMaggio. He was 39; she claimed to be 25 (in fact, she was 28). She held three orchids and asked him to promise, if she died before he did, to put flowers on her grave every week.

After their honeymoon in the Far East she started work on *The Seven Year Itch*, but she was often late and drowsy on the set. She had begun to take barbiturates and her marriage was clearly going on to the rocks.

They split up and the separation was world news. He left for San Francisco, and she appeared on the set the next morning, saying that she felt alive for the first time in days. On 27 October they were divorced.

At Christmas 1954, Marilyn took an apartment in New York and enrolled at Lee Strasberg's famous Actors' Studio. Lee encouraged her to enter psychoanalysis to explore her unconscious and bring true emotion to her acting. About this time she began her relationship with playwright Arthur Miller.

On 1 June, 1955 she attended the première of *The Seven Year Itch*. The film became the

▶ Marilyn at the start of the sixties. By now the actress was in her mid-thirties. She still had her looks, despite being on enormous amounts of prescribed drugs. It was these that were to kill her in August 1962.

summer's biggest grosser, and Marilyn the most photographed person in America. She returned to Hollywood for a new movie, *Bus Stop*, which by June had finished. She joined Arthur Miller while he attended Un-American Activities hearings in Washington DC. He announced that he wanted to go to England that summer and be with his new wife on the set of her picture. The news caused a sensation.

In London. Marilyn was mobbed, but the film set was beset with problems. She was taking large doses of sleeping pills and Miller resented the Strasberg's influence. Still, by November the film was finished and the Millers returned to New York.

They spent the summer of 1957 at Amagansett on Long Island. Arthur began the screenplay of *The Misfits* especially for her though they were barely speaking. She was asked by Billy Wilder to do a new comedy, *Some Like It Hot*. She thought it a suitable stop-gap and began work in July.

CRACKING UP

In no time things turned sour. Jack Lemmon and Tony Curtis were irritated by her lateness and need for 10 to 15 takes of each shot. She began to take pills in the afternoon as well as at night, and Wilder thought that the picture would never be finished. It became one of the most celebrated ever made and the biggest grossing film for 1959.

In July 1960, Marilyn set off for Nevada to film *The Misfits*. Her new therapist, Dr Ralph Greenson, had barbiturates flown in every other day for her. At last the film was finished. Marilyn and Arthur prepared to announce their divorce. To minimize publicity, Marilyn divorced Arthur on 20 January 1961, the day of

It was at this stage that she may have had a brief affair with JFK. On 24 March 1962 they were both Bing Crosby's guests and shared a bedroom. Marilyn always claimed that this was the only weekend they spent in bed together.

Her days developed a routine: a facial, a session with Greenson, a script-reading session with Paula Strasberg, her daily injection of barbiturates, some shopping and another session with Greenson.

On 30 April she appeared for the first time on the set of *Something's Got to Give*. On her return home she collapsed. She stayed in bed, sick, day after day, but announced her intention to appear at JFK's birthday gala in May.

COVER-UP?

On 4 August, Greenson spent the day giving her injections. At 7.30 Joe diMaggio had a pleasant phone conversation with her but, by 7.45, when Peter Lawford rang to invite her to dinner, she was incoherent, only able to mumble 'Goodbye, goodbye'.

By midnight, news had spread that she was dead. Greenson and Murray swore they had to break down doors and smash windows to get into Marilyn's bedroom when they thought something was wrong, yet from the day she had been incarcerated in hospital, Marilyn had never locked a door. There were no locks in the house.

The police were not informed for over four hours, there was no suicide note, and Marilyn was found, naked on her bed with no signs of violence. The only unusual symptom was severe and recent bruising of the colon – suggesting that a fatal dose of drugs was ingested by means of an enema.

For the rest of his life, Joe diMaggio laid flowers at the grave of his beloved each and every week, just as he had promised. He never remarried.

Kennedy's inauguration, and she promptly made a new will, leaving 75 per cent of her estate to Lee Strasberg. *The Misfits* was a critical disappointment and Marilyn grew depressed.

Concerned, her New York therapist drove her to the New York Hospital complex. Marilyn was locked in a padded room for two days and nights. In a state of hysteria, she smuggled out a note to the Strasbergs, begging for help. They did nothing. In desperation, Marilyn contacted Joe diMaggio. He arrived from Florida the next evening and got her release. She stayed with him until March and then went with him to Florida. By April she had returned to Los Angeles.

Marilyn resumed her sessions with Dr Greenson who now decided that outside influences were malevolent. He began to order her to send away her remaining entourage. It was suggested that she play in a film called *Something's Got to Give*. He also ordered her to buy a house, which she did, and then he ordered her to take on a woman called Eunice Murray as her housekeeper, which she also did.

Greenson went on a five-week foreign tour. Free of her tyrant she perked up enough to appear on set for three days in a row, but this was not enough – she was about to be fired. On 19 May a nervous Marilyn began to sing 'Happy Birthday' at the Madison Square Gardens gala in honour of the President's forty-fifth birthday, while the audience cheered.

Next day, she returned to to Los Angeles and the set as though nothing had happened, and also celebrated her birthday – mostly alone. It was too much and she tried to take an overdose.

In July, again Joe diMaggio came to the rescue. They decided to remarry and set a date of 8 August. Older now, they thought that this time they could do better.

One of the immortals – even today fans place fresh flowers on Marilyn's tomb.

Jim Morrison

Outrageous rock star

1943–1971

On 8 December, 1943, James Douglas Morrison was born in Melbourne, Florida, near where his navy father Steve was training to fly. A hero and officer by the end of the war, Steve decided to make a career in the navy. The family, soon with two more children, became comfortably off. Jim, handsome if chubby, enjoyed a typical American boyhood. Intelligent (his IQ was 149), he coasted through school and seemed to have read everything by his teens.

Home life was not idyllic. His mother was domineering, his father an increasingly remote figure, as he climbed higher up the naval ladder. Later Jim would become completely estranged from his parents.

In his senior year at the George Washington High School in Alexandria, Virginia, Jim's mother pressured him to go to college. Finally, she enrolled him in the autumn of 1961 at St Petersburg Junior College. A year later Jim moved to Tallahassee to enrol at Florida State University. In January 1964 he began classes at the UCLA Film School, where he had enrolled against his parents' wishes.

After months of work, in May 1965 Jim's student film was shown at the UCLA film theatre. It was an abstract medley of images and greeted with derision. Jim walked out, pausing only to say, 'I quit.'

He moved to Venice, LA's alternative quarter. The assault on his senses sent Jim into a creative frenzy. He seldom ate, slept for only a few hours a night but was always writing. Songs poured out. 'Hello, I Love You', 'Soul Kitchen' and 'Celebration of the Lizard' were written at this time. When they were ready, he felt compelled to sing his songs himself; the lyrics were too precious, too personal to give to someone else. All he had to do now was find a band.

He ran into pianist Ray Manczarek on Venice beach in August. Jim had appeared

> ## Self-driven to heights of creativity and depths of despair and destruction

with Ray's band, Rick and the Ravens, that June. He told Ray about his songs and Ray asked him to sing one. 'He sat down on the beach and said, "Okay, here's one I got. It's called 'Moonlight Drive'." When I heard the first lines, I said, "Wow, that's it, man. Those are the greatest f...... lyrics I've ever heard. Let's form a band and make a million".' This was just what Jim had in mind. He even had a name for the band: he had chosen The Doors.

Two weeks later, Ray took Jim to his parents' house at Manhattan Beach where Rick and the Ravens rehearsed. Jim's psychedelic lyrics didn't appeal to Ray's brothers, Jim and Rick, but they agreed to join the band. The line-up was completed by the arrival of John Densmore on drums.

Only a fortnight later the band went to World Pacific recording studios on Third Street, Los Angeles. In one or two takes, they recorded six tracks, all songs Jim had written, including 'Moonlight Drive', 'End of the Night' and 'Hello, I Love You'.

The record companies were unimpressed. They didn't like Jim's voice or his songs. The band resumed rehearsals half-heartedly and then Rick and Jim quit. John suggested Robby Krieger, a friend from University High School to help fill the gap. Krieger, Densmore, Manczarek (now Manzarek) and Morrison. The Doors line up was complete.

In the New Year of 1966, after pestering every club-owner on Sunset Strip, they got their first proper gig, playing at the London Fog. The owner's terms were a miserly $5 a night, but it gave them a chance to hone their act.

▶ *Jim Morrison at the height of his powers as the Lizard King. It was his image, and dramatic presence on stage, which transformed The Doors' live performances to total rock theatre.*

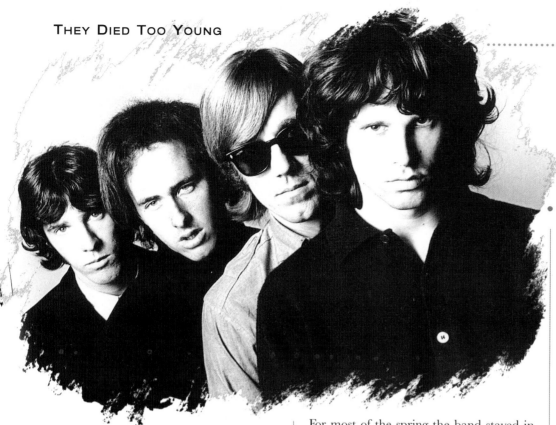

To the band's surprise Bill James of Columbia Records, dropped into the club to see them. He had heard their demo and wanted to sign them. Their joy was short-lived: Columbia soon dropped them, and they were then fired from the Fog.

On the night of their last gig there, the Whisky-A-Go-Go, Sunset Strip's trendiest club, signed them. They played there from mid-May to mid-July 1966. Fired almost every night for their stage antics, they were re-hired because of their following.

JEKYLL AND HYDE

This popular success led to a deal with the small Elektra record label, with an advance of $5,000. The band were flown to New York for the signing and a month of Elektra-organized triumphant gigs at Ondine's disco.

Jim's heavy drinking and drug-assisted explorations of his own mind began to take their toll. About this time he moved in with Pamela Courson, a red-haired 18-year-old who had lived in Laurel Canyon.

In November the band returned to LA, where they started recording their first album at Sunset Sound Studios. Entitled *The Doors*, it was released in January 1967, along with the single 'Break on Through'.

For most of the spring the band stayed in California, playing clubs and concert halls, and arranging an edited-down version of 'Light My Fire'. Jim drank all day. Alcohol was becoming his drug of choice.

By the summer, there was no doubt about the band's success. At the end of July 'Light My Fire' was number 1 where it stayed for a month. In August, the Doors recorded the album *Strange Days*. The advance orders numbered a record 500,000.

Jim's increasingly wild side was displayed at a concert at New Haven, Connecticut, on 5 December 1967. Just before the band were due on stage, Jim argued with a cop, who sprayed mace into his face. The crew rescued him and the show went on.

Halfway through 'Back Door Man', Jim started a rap about what had happened

▶ *Under the pressure of his incessant boozing, the dramatic good looks of Jim's first years of fame gave way to the bloated appearance of his later years. Soon a full beard and dark glasses would complete a look behind which Morrison would try to hide from his fame. The ploy wouldn't work.*

backstage. The audience sat fascinated, as Jim taunted the police at the front. Then the house lights went up and a police lieutenant arrested Jim on stage.

By 1968 Jim was losing interest in being a rock star. Recording the album, *Waiting for the Sun*, had taken forever, partly because Paul Rothchild wanted a technically perfect record, partly because Jim used the studio for partying. John Densmore even quit because of Jim's drunkenness. He came back the next day.

By 1969 The Doors were the biggest group in America. Audiences increasingly expected more of outrageous Jim Morrison. Somehow he had to entertain them beyond their expectations, go further and further out on the edge. And he was drinking more and more.

On 3 March, 1969, the night was hot, and the Dinner Key Auditorium in Miami was packed. A few lines into 'Back Door Man' Jim, now sporting a dark beard, stopped and went into a drunken rap, insulting the audience, calling them idiots. Suddenly he

► *Jim Morrison's exile in Paris became permanent in July 1971, and his grave at the Père La Chaise cemetery in Paris quickly became a shrine. Even in death, it seems, there was no escape – if, of course, Jim Morrison is actually buried there.*

shouted 'Let's get naked', and threw his shirt into the crowd. 'You didn't come here for music,' he continued. 'You came for something else. Something greater than you've ever seen.'

The crowd roared, as Jim intimated he was going to strip. Ray yelled to Vince Treanor, their electrician, who bounded across the stage and just managed to stop him. The stadium went into uproar.

After a few days' holiday in Jamaica, Jim flew home to find that a warrant had been issued for his arrest. Every city in The Doors' upcoming tour cancelled.

At the end of March the FBI charged Jim with unlawful flight, claiming, ridiculously, that he'd left Miami to avoid prosecution He surrendered to the FBI on 4 April, and was released on $5,000 bail.

THE FALL FROM GRACE

The trial was set for April 1970. Anti-Doors hysteria surged. Few venues would host them, even with a $5,000 bond posted against obscenity. Police waited with blank warrants at any shows that did happen.

However, Jim had more time for his poetry. The Doors' next album, *Morrison Hotel*, was a lyrical masterpiece, Jim's strongest work in years. Even the doubters had to acknowledge that The Doors, and Jim especially, could still turn it on.

On Monday 10 August 1970, his trial began in Miami at the Metropolitan Dade County Justice Building. Jim's lawyer, Max Fink, had nearly 100 witnesses lined up to testify that Jim had not exposed himself. The trial staggered on for over a month.

The judge, Murray Goodman, allowed The Doors to play some previously arranged concerts, including one on the Isle of Wight in England, but also refused any evidence about artistic standards, ruling out a main plank of the defence. Jim was found guilty of public exposure and profanity and sentenced to eight months' hard labour at Dade County Jail. He was also fined $500. Jim remained free on $50,000 bail pending an appeal.

Things got worse. Pamela left him. Jimi Hendrix died, followed in quick succession by Janis Joplin. 'I'm gonna be number three,' Jim started telling friends.

Yet he was writing well, producing material for *LA Woman*, including 'Riders on the Storm'. Recorded at the Doors' rehearsal room – in which Jim's vocal booth was a bathroom – the result, exactly suiting the lyrics, had a raw, bluesy feel. It was almost like starting over.

On Jim's 27th birthday, 8 December 1970, he recorded some of his poetry. He liked the result, and his optimism lasted for days. Pam came back to him and a concert in Dallas on 11 December was a success.

Then in New Orleans on the following night, 12 December, Jim crumpled. Witnesses said you could see his will and energy leave him. Jim Morrison never performed with The Doors again.

Early 1971 Jim wanted to get away from everything. Paris was an obvious choice. Pam flew on ahead to find an apartment. Jim spent a few days clearing out his desk at the Doors' office and saying goodbye to friends. He left for Paris on 16 March.

PARIS EXILE

For a while Paris was good. Jim and Pam got on well. A trip to the Mediterranean was idyllic. At the end of June, Jim phoned John Densmore in LA to find out how *LA Woman*, just released, was doing. He placed another call to Bill Siddons, The Doors' manager, and said he was working on some great new songs. Then almost immediately he plunged into despair.

A rumour of Jim's death hit Los Angeles on Monday 5 July. Bill Siddons arrived in Paris on Tuesday morning and found Pam with a sealed coffin and a death certificate, signed by a French doctor. The next day, the Lizard King was buried at the famous *Père La Chaise* cemetery.

What exactly happened may never be known. It seems that Jim died of a heroin overdose – suicidal or accidental. Though he hated heroin, he would try anything, and may have been past caring anyway. The one person who could say, took her secret to the grave. Pamela died of an overdose in 1974.

River Phoenix

Hollywood golden boy

1970–1993

Young hippy Arlyn Dunetz recognized a fellow 'seeker' the moment she met a guy called John on Santa Monica Boulevard, Los Angeles, in 1968. They took to the road, finding work as they could. On 23 August 1970, while living in a commune in Madras, Oregon, Arlyn gave birth to their first child, River Jude.

Still searching for meaning, John and Arlyn joined the Children of God, and became travelling missionaries for the cult. Their daughter Rain Joan of Arc was born in Texas in 1973. Further south Arlyn gave birth to Joaquin. (Rain later changed her name to Rainbow, while Joaquin at the age of four adopted the name Leaf.) In Caracas, Venezuela, Libertad Mariposa, or Liberty Butterfly, was born.

In 1977 the unorthodox family made its way back to the US, settling in Florida where another daughter, Summer Joy, was born. To celebrate their new beginning, the clan took the name Phoenix.

In 1978, when Summer Joy was just three months old, John Phoenix injured his back. He could no longer work, so the children now had to earn. River and Rain, now nine and seven, began to perform in local talent contests, and River walked away with prize after prize. Arlyn began mailing out cuttings about her talented son. The response – a standard reply from the Head of Talent at Paramount – was enough for the family to take to the road and head off to Los Angeles.

Arlyn Phoenix may have been a hippy, but she was hard-nosed. She secured agent Iris Burton to act for the children. His first move was to put River forward for TV commercials, followed by the LA TV audition circuit. The earnest, beguiling child actor made charmed progress, and the jobs came thick and fast.

He was fast conquering TV, but River was born to run and his next move was to the

> **Clean-living star and passionate environmentalist, what went wrong for River Phoenix?**

big screen. His first movie, in 1985, was a science fiction adventure called *Explorers*. By the time he was 15, he had been professionally cute for more than five years. He was probably his family's chief breadwinner. He had never been to school.

If *Explorers* established River as a serious contender in Tinseltown, his next role, won the same year, was one of three films in his career that touched his own

experience. For Rob Reiner's rites of passage movie *Stand By Me*, River was selected from over 300 youngsters to play 13-year-old Chris Chambers, the boy from the wrong side of the tracks.

When this quirky, low-budget production became a surprise hit, River Phoenix was a Hollywood name, and his next movie gave him a lead role with a major star, Harrison Ford. In *The Mosquito Coast* (1986), directed by Australian Peter Weir, Phoenix played elder son Charlie to Harrison Ford's mad inventor father, Allie Fox. Weir also made the right choice in casting charismatic, ugly-attractive young Martha Plimpton as Emily, Allie Fox's daughter. On location in the small country of Belize, River and Martha fell in love.

Mosquito Coast was not a success, and the year following its release was a low point for River. Driven by a need to move from wise-child to adult star, he made two false starts: *A Night in the Life of Jimmy Reardon*, and, in 1987, Richard Benjamin's forgettable spy thriller *Little Nikita*.

'Let's say I took those jobs out of an insecurity, out of a feeling that I might

▶ *Seventeen-year-old River Phoenix in the role of Danny Pope in Sidney Lumet's* Running on Empty. *This was the movie in which River gave notice of his enormous acting talent, and won for himself a Best Supporting Actor nomination at the 1989 Oscars.*

▶ *River on the set of his very first film,* Explorers, *which in 1985 introduced the movie-going public to the child actor who had already carved out a successful career for himself on television.*

never work again,' River later said. But, together, *A Night in the Life* and *Little Nikita* confirmed him as more than a teen idol; he was also sanctified as the green lobby's official pin-up. For River, fame was worth something if he could use it to promote the causes he believed in: the conservation of rain forests, ethical treatment of animals, and care for underprivileged children.

The next project, Sidney Lumet's *Running On Empty*, was the movie that brought River Phoenix back closer to home and confirmed him as a serious heart-throb and an actor to be reckoned with. As always, he played the good son and comforter, the boy whose parents lean on him in troubled times. His performance as Danny Pope was a tour de force, and he was nominated for Best Supporting Actor.

MAKING CHANGES

River could now afford a little time to enjoy himself, so his next bit-part brought a complete change of mood. 'I wanted to do something light, pure entertainment,' he explained, and the part of the young Indiana in *Indiana Jones and the Last Crusade* was ideal. The film was one of the biggest hits of 1989, and now more than ever, River Phoenix was a name on the lips of Hollywood's agents.

Arlyn Phoenix now saw her opportunity to enact the next stage of her plan for her family – a move away from the perils of California. She commented though: 'We couldn't do it until we knew River was famous enough so that we could go away and he would still be offered parts.'

The Phoenix family moved to a 20-acre site near Gainesville, Florida, but River soon moved out to a rented house of his own. The small town found him polite and

unassuming But there were some far-reaching changes going on in the young star's life. His relationship with Martha Plimpton was already under strain.

Meanwhile River and Rainbow returned to their shared childhood love of music and started a band called Aleka's Attic. They played benefits at events like Rock Against Fur and at the fashionable low-rent Hardback Cafe. There River met Suzanne Solgot, a massage therapist four years his senior, who played in an all-girl punk band and who soon moved in to share his house.

Aleka's Attic released only one recording – a song on *Tame Yourself*, a fund-raising compilation for PETA (People for the Humane Treatment of Animals). If, as many were to claim, it was the music scene that introduced River Phoenix to drugs, it was now that his fate was being sealed.

For his next couple of films, Lawrence Kasdan's *I Love You to Death* (1990) and the lead in Nancy Savoca's offbeat *Dogfight* (1991), River was only coasting. It was his next role that truly took him to the edge and from which, it would seem, he never recovered. *My Own Private Idaho*, Gus Van Sant's tender, offbeat, independent movie,

was the film that rocketed River Phoenix to cult stardom.

His performance as a little-rent-boy-lost evoked comparisons with James Dean. He played Mike Waters, a narcoleptic, lone hustler. However River's immersion in his role was so extreme that Van Sant feared the actor was changing into his character. However, this professional dedication won him the Best Actor Award at the Venice Film Festival that year.

THE PRICE OF FAME

Successful though it was, River's personal life was to pay a high price. The truth of what happened on *My Own Private Idaho* is not known. Nobody from that film will talk, but everyone in the film business has now heard the rumours. These suggest that River's heroin use started then, beginning as a professional, as much as a social, experiment – to help generate his brilliant portrait of an addicted, gay, drug-using prostitute.

The next movie must have added to his sense of disillusionment and powerlessness. No doubt, he took it to preserve his nice-kid image after his dive into the gutter. *Sneakers* (1992), directed by Phil Alden Robinson, was a high-tech comedy caper. River despised his own performance.

Unverified tales of drugged, difficult behaviour came in 1993 from the set of River's next film, Peter Bogdanovich's *The Thing Called Love*. A glance at River Phoenix's troubled, gaunt appearance as guitar-wielding cowboy James Wright suggests they were true.

It was whispered knowledge on the film set that River was a mixed-up kid with what was vaguely referred to as a drug problem. Friends say no one with any power in the industry enquired too deeply into just how mixed-up he was for fear of upsetting his money-generating image as a sexy saint. At the end, friends say he just gave in to the drugs, trying to disguise the creeping clues to his abuse.

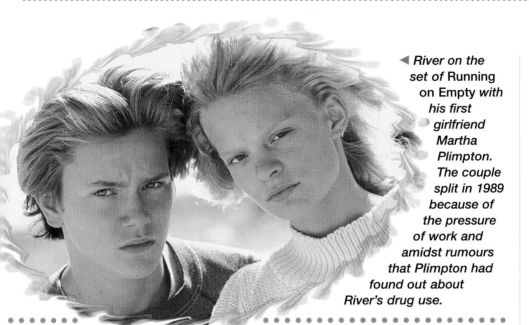

River on the set of Running on Empty *with his first girlfriend Martha Plimpton. The couple split in 1989 because of the pressure of work and amidst rumours that Plimpton had found out about River's drug use.*

The increasingly dark side of River's nature chose his last complete role as Talbot Roe in Sam Shepard's Wild West ghost story, *Silent Tongue* (1993). Most of his time on screen is spent rolling his eyes and howling. A suitably macabre final bow.

For the six weeks just before his death, River was on location in the desert, 300 miles south of Salt Lake City, near a little town called Torrey. He was filming *Dark Blood*, another esoteric movie choice, playing the alternately charming and terrifying character called simply 'Boy'.

THE FATEFUL NIGHT

The location work over, River went back to Los Angeles to start on scenes set inside the hut where Boy lived. He stayed at the Nikko hotel on La Cienega Boulevard. He worked on the Saturday, but he had Sunday off, so he was going to have fun.

Hotel witnesses confirm that River and his friends started partying early that Sunday. Room service delivered drinks and food and noted the chaos, the loud music and the spaced-out look on River's face. They knew it was a drugs high, but they still brought the drinks. At 10.30 pm. he asked for his car be brought round. He and his friends made a rowdy exit from the hotel lobby. Someone else drove while River slumped in the back of the car.

They were on their way to the Viper Club, where River and his friends, some of whom were part of Aleka's Attic, were intending to jam with other musicians. At the club, River was joined by his brother Leaf, his sister Rain and his girlfriend Samantha Mathis. They ordered drinks and a waitress observed that River was stoned on arrival.

Everyone at the Viper on that fateful night agrees on the sequence of events that followed. While sitting at a table, River became terribly ill and began to vomit over himself. His friends took him to the washroom to clean him up. They splashed cold water on his face and tried to stop him trembling; then they got him back to the table. By now he was showing serious signs of an overdose. He began having seizures and then he slumped and slid under the table. Fighting for breath, he asked to be taken to fresh air. Leaf, Rain and Samantha Mathis helped him outside.

▶ *Towards the end of his life, the boyish good looks and hint of innocence had gone from River's face. In its place was a mask of sallow, sick-looking skin and eyes which betrayed more than a hint of suspicion.*

In the dark hours of Halloween, just after 1am, the fragile young star flopped on to the pavement. The seizures started again. After the fifth, he stopped moving. When a four-strong team of paramedics arrived five minutes later, River had 'no pulse and is not breathing'. They provided basic life support and took him to Cedars-Sinai Medical Center a few blocks south. At 1.51am, 20 minutes later, in the emergency room River Phoenix was officially declared dead.

The autopsy confirmed the presence of Valium in River's system – and marijuana and ephedrine. But it was massive doses of heroin and cocaine that killed him. There were no needle marks and no one knew how the drugs had been taken.

A small private memorial service for River Phoenix was held in Hollywood. River's mother spoke the final tribute and laid his memory to rest. Leaf, who had been with him when he died, and his father John chose to remain at home in Florida with his ashes. River had been cremated the week before.

Elvis Presley

Simply – 'The King'

1935–1977

When Elvis Presley died on 16 August 1977, he was the most successful recording artist in the world. He had achieved 63 gold singles, 26 platinum albums, 37 gold albums, and 18 number 1 hits. He had been awarded three Grammys, and had starred in 33 movies. But his start in life could hardly have been less auspicious.

Elvis Aaron Presley was born on 8 January 1935 in his parents' tiny two-roomed shack. His mother Gladys was 22 and his father Vernon was 18. Gladys gave birth to a stillborn boy, later christened Jesse Garon Presley. Thirty-five minutes later, his live twin, Elvis Aaron arrived.

Gladys was distraught at the loss of Jesse, and she clung hysterically to her surviving son. Elvis always thought of Jesse as his missing half. 'If only Jesse were here', he'd say when something good happened.

When Elvis was three, Vernon was arrested for forging a cheque for $100. While he was in prison, his wife and son, already desperately poor, were homeless. Gladys was determined to raise her boy to be honest and to give him every chance to improve himself and escape poverty.

When Elvis was 13, the family were forced to move to Memphis, Tennessee because Vernon had been run out of town by the county sheriff after being caught moonshining (making illegal whiskey). It was here that Elvis began spending time hanging around the blues clubs and listening to the gospel choirs in the churches on the black side of town. He also changed his appearance, dyeing his long blond hair black and buying second-hand sharp, garish clothes.

In the summer of 1953, Elvis graduated, the first Presley to finish high school. Gladys and even Vernon had insisted that their son must get an education.

> ## Like nobody else in history, Elvis was the key to a worldwide musical revolution

Later that year, he set foot for the first time in the recording studio of Sam Phillips' Sun Records. He worked with Phillips off and on for nearly a year until his break came. It was on the night of 5 July 1954, when the young man suddenly started singing an old country blues track, 'That's all right, Mama', that Phillips knew they were on to something and recorded the track. Elvis was on his way.

In May 1955, with his career just taking off, 20-year-old Elvis met and signed up Colonel Tom Parker, the man who was to make him a national phenomenon. Parker began by signing Elvis up to RCA, and the first recordings were made in Nashville in January 1956. 'Heartbreak Hotel' was released two weeks after it was recorded, and 'Don't Be Cruel', and 'Hound Dog' soon followed. Elvis became the hottest singer in America.

Parker knew the power of the media and the publicity that could be gained from a bit of controversy, so he paid dozens of girls to 'faint' at Elvis' performances in early 1956. His appeal to American youth increased in direct proportion to their parents' disapproval.

Elvis was dazed at his sudden, massive success: 'Everything's happened so fast in the past year and a half, I'm all mixed up,' he said. Parker then moved him into television. As his career took off, so did the backlash. His performance of 'Hound Dog' on the Milton Berle Show caused outrage and journalists asked him how he felt about corrupting the nation's youth.

The next step had to be the movies. Parker negotiated a Hollywood deal, and *Love Me Tender* (1956) soon followed. It was critically panned, but the audiences loved

▶ *Elvis as the young rocker, before the draft took him into the US Army. His moves, his swagger and his unique feeling for a song created a revolution in popular music.*

it. As his fame spread, Elvis decided to find a new home. He moved the whole family, including some cousins and friends, into a 14-room, $100,000 mansion in July 1957. Graceland represented everything he had aspired to: he even had the outside repainted so that his Memphis neighbours could see it glowing in the dark.

In March 1958, Elvis was midway through the filming of his fourth movie, when the Colonel rang to tell him he had been

drafted into the army. He was shocked and worried about his career, but could do nothing. Some weeks later he left for Fort Hood training camp in the state of Texas.

Soon after this Gladys fell ill with hepatitis, and was sent to hospital in Memphis. Her condition deteriorated so much that Vernon arranged for Elvis to come and see her. He was shocked by his mother's appearance, but she insisted that he go home to get some rest. He went out with some friends and then to his room with his current girlfriend. Gladys died on the night of 14 August 1958.

Her sudden death changed Elvis. He never forgave himself for not being with her when she died. The main focus of his life was gone, and from that point on, he was on a collision course with disaster.

PRISCILLA

In September 1958, Elvis was shipped to Bad Nauheim in West Germany. There he met 14-year-old Priscilla Beaulieu, whom Elvis thought, bore a striking resemblance to his late mother. In his few remaining months as a soldier he saw her practically every night, until the couple had to part.

He came home to Memphis on 2 March 1960, and was immediately besieged by fans. The Colonel had been working hard to keep Elvis' career alive while he was in Germany. Two albums, *Loving You* and *King Creole*, had gone platinum and his singles had gone straight into the top ten.

▲ *Colonel Tom Parker took the raw talent of a young southern boy, and promoted it from R 'n' B songs to television and movies. But somewhere along the way, the innocence and love of the music died.*

The Colonel drew up a busy schedule for Elvis, with the intention of plunging him straight back into the spotlight. Plans were also made for the next movie – *G.I Blues*.

Within two years, Elvis was feeling isolated, restless and moody. To his horror, his father had remarried, he missed his mother and was angry with everyone. He gorged himself on junk food and gobbled down pills. There was only one way out of his depression. He sent for Priscilla. Her first visit lightened his mood, and by the end of 1963 he decided he wanted to install her in Graceland permanently. Priscilla moved in in early 1964.

It was not long before tension began to grow between the couple. Elvis' mood swings and depression returned. He took more and more pills. Despite this, pressure mounted to make his relationship with Priscilla official. He finally relented, and the two were married in Las Vegas on 1 May 1967. Within weeks of the honeymoon Elvis was womanizing while Priscilla waited for him at Graceland. Even the news that she was pregnant did not stop him. Lisa Marie Presley, Elvis' sole heir, was born on 1 February 1968.

FINAL CHALLENGES

Elvis was itching to perform again and the Colonel agreed. It was to be the beginning of a decade of non-stop touring. The Colonel booked him into a gruelling schedule of performances: 168 in 1971, 156 in 1972 and 169 in 1973, right across America.

Clad in his rhinestone-encrusted stage suits, Elvis threw himself into his live performances with enthusiasm. Priscilla meanwhile, frustrated and lonely, filed for divorce, which eventually came through on 9 October 1973. The divorce affected Elvis badly, and he was also suffering from the sheer number of performances he was giving. On stage he began to become a caricature of himself. All he had to do to keep everyone happy was to be Elvis Presley, and gradually he began to lose track of himself in the myth.

He was fed up, lonely and increasingly paranoid about his safety. He carried guns around with him and even wore a bullet-proof vest on stage. He gorged on food, gaining weight, and took masses of pills.

Every concert he did, whatever state he was in, was still a sell-out, but it was as though he had no goals left. He had the

windows at Graceland covered, blocking out the sunlight, and read spiritual books of every denomination to try to find meaning in his success. He squandered his looks, his sexuality, his talent, his wealth, and no-one was powerful enough, or perhaps cared enough, to stop him.

THE LAST YEARS

Elvis spent the last two years of his life lonely and in pain. He had an enlarged heart, a twisted colon, a damaged kidney, and a serious prescribed-drug addiction. His weight soared to 250 pounds, he began to forget words on stage, and his performances bordered on self-parody. By summer 1977, Elvis was completely lost and his sense of reality utterly distorted: he was incoherent and rambling and full of self-loathing.

On the last night of his life, he played racquetball at four in the morning, as usual, then went to bed to read while his latest girlfriend Ginger Alden slept next to him. He called down to his aunt for some water and his medication at 6 am, saying he could not sleep. Ginger woke at 2 pm, on 16 August 1977, to find him face down on the bathroom floor. The paramedics were called, and he was taken to Memphis Memorial Hospital, but all efforts to revive him failed.

The king of rock 'n' roll was dead, and the world could not believe it. Rumours that it was not true began almost at once and still remain in circulation.

The body was taken to a Memphis funeral home, and laid out at Graceland the next day. Thousands of people paid their respects, and radio stations everywhere played his records back to back.

The coffin was first laid to rest at Forest Hill mausoleum next to Gladys, but when

▲ *The shrine visited by millions of adoring fans, Elvis' grave in the meditation garden at Graceland. He is buried next to his mother.*

three masked men attempted to steal the body to try to prove the death had been faked, both coffins were quickly brought back to Graceland and buried in the meditation garden. An eternal flame was lit, and the following words were inscribed on his grave by his father Vernon:
'HE WAS A PRECIOUS GIFT FROM GOD, WE CHERISHED AND LOVED DEARLY.
HE HAD A GOD GIVEN TALENT THAT HE SHARED WITH THE WORLD.'

Elvis' entire fortune was left in trust to Lisa Marie and in 1982 Colonel Parker was compelled to relinquish all rights to the estate. To date, Elvis Presley's record sales exceed 1.5 billion.

◄ *Elvis in the 1970s. The will to perform was still there, but the man was rapidly being destroyed by the myth. The years of a destructive lifestyle were taking their toll.*

Ayrton Senna

Grand Prix Champion

1960–1994

Ayrton Senna da Silva was born in São Paulo, Brazil, on 21 March 1960. His father, Milton ran a car parts factory. Milton made him a 1-hp go-kart when he was four, and by the age of 13, he was competing at the Interlagos professional kart-racing track.

He won the Brazilian Championship four times and, in 1977, the South American Championship, in the 100cc international category. A dedicated driver, he was not friendly to his rivals. Winning was all.

At 18 he headed off to Europe, the heart of international motor racing. He had booked a season's racing with the DAP kart factory in Milan and tested karts for a while at the international track at Parma

In his first year, Senna came sixth in the championships. He tried for the title again in 1979, but didn't win. In 1980 he had a last try at Nivelles in Belgium, but only made second place.

Now 20, he was near the top of the karting world. He could stay and hope to become champion or move on. In spring 1981, he was in Britain, hoping for a Formula Ford 1600 drive for the season. He settled in Snetterton in Norfolk, with his wife, Liliane, and arranged a season with the Van Diemen team. Three competitions were open to him: the P&O, the Townsend Thoresen (TT) and the RAC.

On 1 March 1981, Senna competed in a round of the P&O Championship at Brands Hatch. He was halfway up the grid when the race started, but clawed his way to fifth position by the end. A week after his debut, he was at Thruxton for the first round of the TT Championship, and came in third. At Brands Hatch, in the second round of the TT, in the wet, he won.

Shortly afterwards, Dennis Rushen, who ran a 2000 Van Diemen team offered Senna the British and European 2000

> **Even superb racing skills and natural courage were not enough at Imola in 1994**

season. Senna went on to win six races in a row, and by the end of 1981 he had taken both the RAC and TT Championships. Everybody thought that he'd be back for 1982 in Formula 3, but he was unable to find a sponsor.

Senna returned at the beginning of the 1982 season. He didn't bother with long practice sessions. He got straight into his car and began winning.

Soon, the McLaren and Toleman teams were offering a sponsored Formula 3 drive but Senna turned them down. He still wanted to shine in Formula 2000. He won the British and the European 2000 Championship at Jyllandsring, Denmark, going from unknown to double champion in Formula 2000 in a year.

Now he could graduate to Formula 3. Dick Bennetts of West Surrey Racing, offered him a drive for 1983.

The 20 rounds of the Marlboro Formula 3 Championship took place over six circuits. The first race was at Silverstone on 6 March 1983, to which WSR sent Senna in a Ralt-Toyota. A Ralt-Toyota, prepared by Eddie Jordan Racing, was also driven by the hopeful Martin Brundle. Senna won with a 7-second lead over Brundle.

At Thruxton he won again. A week later at Silverstone, he was beaten off the start by Brundle, but overtook him. On 30 May, he beat Brundle by 10 seconds at Silverstone, his tenth victory in a row. Williams approached him for a test Formula 1 run.

Two weeks later, Brundle switched from British to European tyres, which gave him

▶ *Ayrton Senna: the winner of three world Grand Prix Championships, was a driver of immense daring and almost uncanny racing skills. His luck, however, was to run out during the 1994 Imola Grand Prix.*

a little extra speed. Brundle got pole position, and won after Senna spun off.

This failure led to mistakes in ensuing races. By 2 October Brundle was ahead in points, 123 to 122. There were only two races left, the Macau Grand Prix and Thruxton. At Macau, Senna had pole position, hared off into the distance, and held the lead to the chequered flag.

He had tested for some Formula 1 teams, meanwhile, including Marlboro McLaren and Brabham, but signed to Toleman. Lotus had been interested, but wanted to keep a British driver, Nigel Mansell.

FORMULA 1

The first real test for the Toleman team was the Monaco Grand Prix. Senna doggedly pushed his way up the ranking: ninth on the first lap, third by lap 16, and by the end of lap 19, only Alain Prost was in front. By lap 31, there were only 7.5 seconds between them, but Prost had been signalling for the race to stop. As Prost slowed towards the end of 32, Senna zipped past, but the positions were decided on the basis of lap 31.

At the end of 1984, he left Toleman for Lotus, quickly becoming the team's focus.

His first race was in Brazil, where he was in third position when his electrics gave up. At Estoril in Portugal, despite heavy rain, he came in first – his first Grand Prix win.

In 1985 he had pole position seven times. At the end of the season's championship he was in fourth position, but with 55 points, over 50 per cent better than 1984.

The first race of the 1987 season, Senna's third with Lotus, in Brazil, was not a great success. At Imola he could not outpace Mansell. At Spa they duelled again, until on a corner the two cars locked together, and spun off. Mansell got back on the track and as far as lap 17 before giving up. He then went to the Lotus pit and grabbed Senna by the throat. It took three mechanics to pull him off.

Senna began racing in a way that would accumulate points, a strategy that paid off. By the seventh Grand Prix of the season, he led by 31 points to Mansell's and Piquet's 30. Even so, he had decided that Lotus were not going to bring him the Championship and signed to McLaren.

At Rio de Janeiro on 3 April 1988, his first race with McLaren, he had pole, but was

later disqualified. Coming in first from team-mate Prost at Imola made up for this. Later, in the Monaco Grand Prix, Senna claimed pole but lost concentration and hit the barrier. Prost won, as he did in Mexico. At Montreal the two McLarens paced each other in front, with Senna making his winning bid on lap 19. At Detroit on 19 June, Senna led from start to finish.

It was the McLarens again at the French Grand Prix: Prost from Senna. It was becoming a one-team championship. After another Senna win at Silverstone in July, the tension grew: Senna and Prost were level with 66 points. After a win at Spa on 26 August, Senna had a three-point lead.

BATTLE OF THE GIANTS

They duelled maniacally at Estoril on 25 September. Prost won, and Senna dropped to sixth. After this, there was real anger between them, and they ceased to act as a team. Prost was now five points ahead, with 81. After Jerez, Prost stayed on top, with 84 to Senna's 79. Only two races remained.

At Suzuka, Senna's twelfth pole of the season, he stalled at the start. His engine finally caught, but he was in fourteenth place. By lap 2 he had made sixth, and by lap 15 he was second. Finally in lap 27 he roared past Prost on a straight. The lead was his, never to be lost. He was World Champion. Adelaide didn't matter.

The new season started amicably, but at Imola the animosity revived. Senna won, but had overtaken Prost approaching a bend. Senna argued that he had done so on a straight, but Prost said it was on the bend itself, a move they had informally agreed not to do. The McLaren manager

◀ *Senna began his Formula 1 career in 1984, after spectacularly successful years racing in Formula Ford and Formula 3 competitions. It was an apprenticeship he was not to forget during his victorious glory years in Formula 1.*

The gates outside the headquarters of Williams Racing in England become an impromptu shrine, as crowds of fans leave flowers in memory of one of the greatest drivers motor sport had ever seen.

tried to smooth things over, but it was too late. The drivers were no longer on speaking terms. Prost signed to drive for Ferrari the following season.

1990 began with a win at Phoenix. In Brazil the spark returned, as Senna felt he was racing for the nation. His confidence and awareness came back. At Spa, he and Prost had a public reconciliation.

As the season went on, Senna established a clear lead. He was on his 51st pole at Suzuka, but for Senna and Prost the race was over in 10 seconds. It was almost a rerun of 1989. Prost was furious and claimed that Senna had pushed him off the track. At Adelaide, Senna hit a barrier. It didn't matter, he was Champion again.

In 1991 he seemed less hectic. He was accumulating points without expecting to dominate every race. Seven wins were enough to beat off the Mansell challenge and he had his third Championship.

The 1992 season was miserable. The new Williams-Renaults of Mansell and Ricardo

Patrese outclassed McLaren. At the end of the year he was fourth, behind Mansell (108 points), Patrese (56) and Michael Schumacher (53). 1993 was worse. Senna had hoped to drive for Williams, but they took Prost. At the end of the year, Prost announced his retirement; Senna could now move to Williams.

Each time he had changed team his successes had increased. But at Imola, ill-fortune hung over the race. Rubens Barrichello was injured in practice and Roland Ratzenberger crashed and died shortly afterwards. Senna was deeply affected and did not take part in the

practice that day. He told his fiancée, (his wife had divorced him) that he did not want to race the following day.

IMOLA, 1 MAY 1994

There was a crash as the race began and it had to be restarted. Senna led, with Schumacher on his tail. On lap 7, he reached the Tamburello corner, but instead of taking the bend, he just went straight on, hitting a concrete wall at over 160 mph. The car was demolished, and Senna sat motionless. A helicopter flew him to the Maggiore hospital, but his skull was crushed beyond medical skill. Brain death had happened at the wall. Life ceased at 6.40 pm.

Brazil declared three days of national mourning. At the funeral, on 5 May, the weeping crowds were immense. Prost was one of the pall bearers. Before the race, they had shaken hands and Prost had said maybe they might be friends again in the future. It was not to be.

If world motor sport was shocked at Senna's tragic death, then his fellow Brazilians went into national mourning for one of their most treasured heroes. On its return to his homeland, Senna's body was given a full state funeral.

Rudolph Valentino

The Great Lover

1895–1926

On 6 May 1895 Rodolpho Alfonzo Raffaelo Pierre Filiberto Guglielmi di Valentina d'Antonguolla was born to Giovanni and Donna Beatrice Guglielmi in Castellaneta, Italy.

Rodolpho's first ambition was to get out of the village, and his first step came after his father's death when he was 11. Finding him difficult, his mother sent him to school in nearby Taranto. The novelty soon wore off and he set his sights first on Rome, then on America. He pressured his mother until she gave him the money his father had set aside for his education. On 9 December 1913, he set sail for the United States.

Arriving in New York two days before Christmas, he settled with an Italian family in West 49th Street. He began to learn English and took several menial jobs. In six months his English was good enough for him to move from the Italian quarter, and he got a series of gardening jobs. By the summer of 1914, though, he was homeless, sleeping rough in Central Park.

Then Rodolpho got lucky with a job as a busboy in an Italian restaurant. His fellow workers introduced him to New York's dance halls. With his Latin looks, graceful physique and hypnotic eyes, he was an instant success. Soon earning $6 a day he happily extended his services with 'love breaks' in his dressing-room for a tip or gift.

He became an accomplished dancer and was hired as resident tango-dancer at Maxim's, a high-class establishment.

There Rodolpho met Bianca de Saulles, heiress, and wife of Jack de Saulles, a prominent New Yorker. They began a passionate year-long affair.

As Rodolpho's love for Bianca became more intense, he decided to become a legitimate professional dancer. Meanwhile, he and Bianca manoeuvred de Saulles into adultery, the only grounds for divorce. Their plan succeeded, but de Saulles set

From peasant to gigolo and from dancer to adored heart-throb of the silent screen

up Rodolpho with a blackmail charge. This was dropped, but Rodolpho feared deportation and got out of town until things died down. In his absence, in August 1917, Bianca shot and killed Jack over custody of their child, and Rodolpho, fearful of his involvement, headed West.

In San Francisco he landed a part in the chorus line of a show, making some good contacts. Norman Kerry, a young actor just beginning to make it in Hollywood, was one. He put Rodolpho up while he made the rounds, seeking $5 a day parts.

Rodolpho's first break, a dancer in the film *Alimony*, came through Kerry. Soon after, the star Mae Murray and her husband, director Bob Leonard, spotted Rodolpho dancing. She insisted he play the leading man in her new film, *The Big Little Person*. This was followed by another Murray film, *The Delicious Little Devil*.

His next picture, *A Society Sensation*, was with Carmel Meyers. He also made *All Night* with Meyers and was given a pay rise. After this, Rodolpho's luck took a turn for the worse, and he was reduced to dancing in the prologue to warm up the audience for a D.W. Griffith film *Scarlet Days*.

Rodolpho accepted an invitation to a small party at the Ship's Café in honour of the film star, Alla Nazimova. Knowing of the de Saulles scandal, she snubbed him. He left the party in shame, but luckily Hollywood was full of support. Aspiring starlet, Jean Acker, one of Nazimova's lesbian circle, expressed her sympathy. He was besotted with her. A few days later, he

▶ *Valentino in perhaps his most famous role, in the lead of* The Sheik. *The film broke all previous box office records, and generated an unparalleled level of mass hysteria amongst his millions of fans worldwide.*

proposed marriage and, caught up in the romance of the situation, she agreed.

MIXED BLESSINGS

Eager to consummate the marriage, he was bewildered and hurt when his wife, faced with the prospect of heterosexual sex, shut him out of her apartment on their wedding night. The only good thing to come of the marriage was Jean's suggestion that he change his name to Rudolph Valentino.

Meanwhile June Mathis, top screenwriter of the day, head-hunted Valentino to play Julio, the Latin hero in *The Four Horsemen of the Apocalypse* by Vicente Blasco Ibanez.

With eight months to wait before the première, Valentino made another film with Metro, *Uncharted Seas*. The ever-unpredictable Nazimova visited him on set, wanting him for her new film *Camille*. She introduced him to Natacha Rambova, her new protégée. Born Winifred Shaughnessy in Salt Lake City, Utah, Natacha was rich, cosmopolitan, strong-willed, manipulative,

and ambitious. He was enthralled with her, and she used this power to dominate him. He became her 'project'. He was her career and she was to become his greatest love and his worst nightmare.

In March 1921, *The Four Horsemen* opened and was hailed as a masterpiece. Valentino asked for a rise. Metro offered only $50 a week more. On Natacha's insistence, he quit. The gamble paid off. Jesse Lasky of Paramount asked him to play the lead in a film of the new bestseller *The Sheik*. Despite Natacha's disapproval, he took the role.

Reviews of *The Sheik* wrote it off as mere romance – but that was just what made women flock to see it. It broke all box-office records, amassing $2,000,000 in two years and a cumulative audience of over 125,000,000 people. Valentino became the screen's first male sex-symbol. Crowds mobbed him wherever he went.

The Valentinos' divorce was heard in the midst of all this mania, in November 1921. Jean sued for maintenance and he filed for divorce, as the marriage had not been consummated. She admitted that they had never slept together, and left the court in the arms of a woman friend. The divorce was granted in Valentino's favour, due to her desertion.

Valentino made two films with Paramount right after *The Sheik*: *Moran of the Lady Letty* and *Beyond the Rocks*, with Gloria

◀ As a heart-throb of the silent screen, Rudolph Valentino, ex-dancer and New York gigolo, had no equal. His performance as Julio in the 1921 hit film The Four Horseman of the Apocalypse *launched him on his big-time Hollywood career.*

▶ A classic Valentino publicity shot of the early twenties. Even in these early years, the Hollywood star system was already sophisticated enough to groom and mould a humble Italian immigrant and turn him into the most desirable man in the world.

Swanson. He was now earning $1,000 a week. Natacha's presence on the set made everyone involved miserable and Valentino himself became hypercritical and unco-operative, demanding artistic recognition.

Valentino's 'artistic needs' were appeased by the offer of the role of Juan Gallardo in another Ibanez drama, *Blood and Sand*. He was ecstatic, as it was his favourite type of role, with elaborate costumes, semi-nude scenes to show off his body and bullfighting scenes to display his manliness.

REMARRIAGES

Natacha and Rudolph went to Mexico and were married on 13 May 1922 in Mexicali. They then headed to Palm Springs for a honeymoon only to discover that the law required a year's delay after divorce, so their marriage was bigamous. Valentino was arrested and thrown in jail.

To his horror, his lawyers and the studio advised him to testify that they had not slept together since the wedding – in effect, to announce that he, the Great Lover, had not consummated either of his marriages. As the alternative was probably a one- to five-year jail sentence, he obeyed the lawyers. The charges were dropped.

Paramount claimed that the trial was worth $1 million in free publicity, but the cost to Valentino was public humiliation. Immediately after his next film, *The Young Rajah*, he went east to join Natacha, who 'helped' him prepare a statement that he was leaving Paramount due to artistic differences. The case went to court, which decided in Paramount's favour. He either had to honour his contract or retire from the film business until February 1924. Valentino chose retirement.

Entrepreneur, S. George Ullmann was one of many following the case. Knowing the couple's financial difficulties, he made an offer: $7,000 a week for a dance tour to endorse the Mineralava Beauty Clay Company's cosmetics. It was at this time that Valentino and Natacha were finally married, on 14 March 1923, in Crown Point, Indiana. They then began the tour, which was an enormous success.

Ullmann became Valentino's personal manager. He cleared debts and negotiated a new deal with Paramount requiring two more films for them before Valentino joined a new company. These, *Monsieur Beaucaire* and *A Sainted Devil*, were disasters. Natacha's interference was even worse. Paramount was glad to hand over its 'nightmare' to Ritz-Carlton Pictures.

The new contract gave the couple artistic control. Their first film was written by Natacha and set in medieval Spain. She insisted on a trip to Spain for authentic props. The couple spent $100,000 on antiques alone, and the pre-production costs sent Ritz-Carlton into liquidation.

The couple had an urgent meeting with Ullmann, who had an offer for Valentino from United Artists: $1 million a year, with a strict exclusion of Natacha. While she protested and hurled abuse, Valentino reached his limit and stood up to her. He signed the contract, and effectively ended his marriage.

Valentino's first film for United Artists was *The Eagle*. At its New York première in November 1925, five bodyguards had to walk him from his hotel to the limousine; the reception was more hysterical than ever. He was still the champion of the box office.

On 10 November 1925, Valentino applied for US citizenship, the same day that Natacha returned from Europe and two days after she had applied for divorce in Paris. In January 1926 the divorce was granted.

A FREE MAN

For the first time since he became a sex symbol, Valentino was a single man. His fans were in overdrive, and his film colleagues were not much better. The actress Pola Negri became his constant companion. His reputation as the Great Lover was enhanced by his next film, *The Son of the Sheik*. It exploited the legend of Valentino the Love God, and it was an incredible hit.

He set off east to publicize it and began a round of wild partying in New York. The summer was a whirl of parties and personal

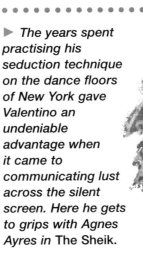

► *The years spent practising his seduction technique on the dance floors of New York gave Valentino an undeniable advantage when it came to communicating lust across the silent screen. Here he gets to grips with Agnes Ayres in* The Sheik.

appearances, and the pace began to tell. Valentino had been suffering from stomach pains for some time, but had insisted that it was just indigestion.

On 14 August 1926 he went to an all-night party held in his honour. Next morning Ullmann found him writhing on the floor of his hotel room. He was rushed to New York's Polyclinic Hospital and operated on for acute appendicitis and gastric ulcer.

A few days later, he was feeling much better and said that he would be able to leave the hospital within a few days. The doctors took this rapid cessation of pain to be a worrying sign and did another examination. Complications had set in, including poisoning of the wall of the heart. On Monday morning he awoke in great pain and was given morphine. By the next morning he was in a coma; two priests administered the last rites. Shortly before noon on 23 August 1926, 'with a priest's crucifix pressed to his lips', Rudolph Valentino died 'without pain' at the age of 31.

The star's final appearance was even more hysterical than those when he was alive. Nearly 100,000 emotional fans caused a near-riot as they tried to view the body. He was laid to rest on 7 September 1926 in June Mathis's family crypt at the Hollywood Cemetery, while blossoms were dropped from a plane.

Sid Vicious

Sex Pistols' guitarist

1957–1979

John Simon Ritchie, who would become Sid Vicious, was born on 10 May 1957 in London. His mother, Ann Beverley, had a hard childhood, abandoned by her unmarried mother, marrying young, and having Sid by another man, John Ritchie. She used to call her son Simon Ritchie, though to childhood friends he was John Beverley (Beverley being Ann's second husband's name). She was a firm member of the hippy movement while John was a child and took him on the hippy trail when he was ten. She was also no stranger to drugs.

John developed an early awareness of the hardship in his neighbourhood, and although no fighter, he was able to take care of himself. He also learned a disrespect for authority, although he was close to his mother. He left school at 15 and worked in a clothing factory, before taking a photography course at college.

In 1973 John Beverley met John Lydon at Hackney Technical College. They teamed up with John Gray and John Wardle (later bassist Jah Wobble). Lydon renamed Beverley Sid, after his pet hamster, which was also called Vicious.

The people that Lydon and Sid gathered around them had all the attitude in the world, and all they needed was a direction.

Meanwhile, Malcolm McLaren and his partner Vivienne Westwood had opened a shop at 430 King's Road, London in 1971. By 1973 he had renamed the shop Sex, and McLaren and Westwood began to stock rubber and leather clothes which they sold to the bored teenagers who had started to hang out on the King's Road. Among these kids were members of a band called The Strand: Steve Jones, Paul Cook and Wally Nightingale.

Jones used to harass McLaren about the band, until, at the end of 1973, he found them some rehearsal space. A note of

Fate cursed Sid Vicious with an inner drive to headlong self-destruction

musical ability was injected into the band at this time with the addition of Glen Matlock, who was working in the shop, on bass. Cook was the drummer, Jones took the vocals, and Nightingale was on guitar.

Throughout 1974 The Strand continued rehearsing, and when McLaren left for New York in November he had already formulated the idea for a band which would be a promotional tool for the shop.

When he came back in the spring of 1975, he brought some valuable ideas. He went to work on The Strand, getting rid of Nightingale and putting Jones on guitar.

In August 1975 Bernie Rhodes, a friend of McLaren's and soon-to-be manager of The Clash, saw John Lydon and invited him to Sex. It was instantly obvious to McLaren that he had the front to lead a band, and an audition got him the job.

By November 1975 the band was ready for their first gig at St Martins School of Art, and Lydon had a new name, chosen by Jones because of the state of Lydon's teeth: Johnny Rotten. The name Sex Pistols was chosen just before the gig. They played five songs before the power was cut off.

It was soon apparent that booking concerts would be a problem, and they succeeded for a while by simply arriving at venues and saying that they had been told they could play. The Sex Pistols spent about nine months' gigging up and down the country, gathering small numbers of converts at each venue, led by Sid, their number one fan. He was encouraged in his outlandishness by McLaren, who saw him as a useful figurehead.

Sid was also determined to be in a band. He taught himself the rudiments of the bass guitar in one night, with the help of the Ramones album and a supply of speed. At the 'Punk festival' in September he was the drummer for Siouxsie and the Banshees' first gig at the 100 Club. He also

wrote some lyrics with titles such as 'Piece of Garbage', 'Brains on Vacation' and the particularly offensive 'Belsen was a Gas'.

HITTING THE HEADLINES

As Sid Vicious was honing his Punk persona, the Sex Pistols were being led by McLaren towards a record deal. He touted a demo tape made in July 1976 around the major companies. EMI offered a £40,000 advance, in a two-year contract which was drawn up in a single day. The deal was signed on 8 October 1976.

The Pistols had seemingly pulled some very expensive wool over the eyes of a major record company, and the tabloids latched on to the heady mixture of hype and truth. The next steps were the release of a single 'Anarchy in the UK', and a drunken appearance on prime time television which jammed the phone lines to the studios, and brought headlines in the press. From then on the Sex Pistols were the main act in a media circus.

The uproar meant that the Pistols' tour, due to begin three days later, was hit by cancellations. Only three of the planned 19 dates were played and an estimated £10,000 was lost, although 'Anarchy in the UK' was in the top thirty at number 27. Unable to play in the UK, they made a short tour of Holland, gaining 'Rotten sick at Heathrow' headlines. It was the final straw for EMI. The Sex Pistols were dropped from the label, although they went with the recording advance and publishing money still in their hands.

The last Dutch gig was also Matlock's final show with the band. Antagonism between

▲ *Sid plays the blood-stained, self-mutilating rock star, while Johnny Rotten mouths off. The two had been friends since 1973, and it was largely through Rotten that Sid became the Sex Pistols' final member.*

him and Rotten got too much for him, and when Sid started to turn up for rehearsals he decided to go. Sid became the Pistols bassist and started to live the life he thought vital to someone of his rock status.

Before Sid could show himself on stage in his new role, there was the matter of a new record company to sort out. The Sex Pistols signed up with A&M Records on

9 March 1977 for £75,000, with a symbolic signing outside Buckingham Palace the day after. It turned into a day-long public relations disaster for the record company, and on 16 March, just a week after signing, A&M and the Sex Pistols parted company. In a little over six months the Pistols had managed to take £125,000 from two major record companies.

FATAL ATTRACTION

Sid joined the Sex Pistols at the same time as beginning the other great involvement of his life, his meeting with American Nancy Spungen, who, at 19, was a year younger than him. She had been in therapy since childhood and had attempted suicide twice. She was notorious on the American rock circuit as a groupie and heroin addict. Sid's character was no match for Nancy's sex and drugs combination, but she was the love of his life and the two soon became inseparable. She helped to persuade him that he was the star of the Sex Pistols and he soon started to act like it.

The Pistol's next record contract was with Virgin Records. On 12 May a £50,000 advance was agreed and signed. There was now a rush on to get 'God save the Queen' released in time for the prime marketing period of the Silver Jubilee week

of 9 June. It was on sale from 27 May, and went into the charts at number 11, but television and radio stations refused to advertise it and major retailers refused to stock it.

A media backlash was not slow in coming. The press resumed its Pistol-packed headlines, and the country as a whole poured a stream of hatred on to the band. The Pistols were forced to lie low, and a brief tour of Scandinavia was quickly arranged. Before they left, 'Pretty Vacant' was rush-released on 2 July 1977.

The Pistols travelled to Copenhagen on 13 June for the start of a successful two week tour. Sid was not taking any hard drugs for the duration, and his live playing was proving better than his studio work: the Pistols had to bring back Matlock for recording tracks for the planned album.

Trying to continue the live exposure, the band set about an undercover tour of England, called the SPOTS tour (Sex Pistols On Tour Secretly). This took them into September, during which time Sid had returned to Nancy and his drug habit, while the album *Never Mind the Bollocks* was coming together. The last recording the band as a whole would make, it was successfully released on the 28th, entering the charts at number 1.

They now prepared to go on an extended tour, taking in America and Europe. Half the English gigs were cancelled, and there was frustration over visas for America because of their various criminal records. Only when their new American label, Warners, agreed to pay a surety of $1 million were the visas granted.

On 3 January 1978, the Sex Pistols flew to New York on a two-week visa, where they

were taken under the wing of Warner representatives determined to keep the $1 million bond safe. The Pistols caught an onward flight for the first gig at Atlanta, where they bombed. By the time the Pistols reached San Francisco for the 14 January show they had been banned from several hotel chains, and refused work permits for the next stage of the tour in Finland. The next gig was at Winterland, the biggest venue the Pistols had ever played, with a capacity of 5,000, and it was a disaster.

THE END OF EVERYTHING

Two days later, the Sex Pistols imploded, and Rotten, Jones and Cook all quit. Sid called Rotten with a garbled message to the effect that he, too, was finished with the Pistols. Later, he took a cocktail of drugs which put him in a coma and led to his immediate hospitalization on his arrival in New York.

Sid and Nancy settled down in the city, and immediately returned to their drug-based existence. Sid was persuaded to go to Paris, where he recorded 'My Way'. He also recorded versions of the Eddie Cochran songs 'C'mon Everybody' and 'Something Else'. At the end of August that year he played a 'Sid Sods Off' gig at Camden's Electric Ballroom, before moving to New York for good.

In New York, Sid and Nancy took room 100 at the Chelsea Hotel on West 23rd Street, but their hopes of a fresh start were soon dashed by their continuing drug use and constant violence, as well as the city's refusal to accept them as the stars which they proclaimed themselves to be.

There was a concert in September 1978, with the remnants of the New York Dolls and the Clash's Mick Jones backing Sid. However, by October he was becoming more and more isolated.

In the early morning of 12 October, Sid woke from a drug-induced sleep to find Nancy lying in a pool of blood under the bathroom sink, with his hunting knife in her side. The police arrived, he admitted to killing her and was charged with second

◀ *For all his self-promoting image of hatred, anger and contempt, ironically without intention, Sid Vicious ultimately directed his aggression on the love of his life and his life itself.*

▲ *For each 'shocking' concert that actually took place, several others were invariably cancelled.*

degree murder. Several versions of the events leading to this outcome would be put forward, but the actual details as described by Sid are that earlier that night, while waiting for drugs to be delivered, he went around banging on other doors in the hotel. He was hit on the nose by the night attendant, and when he went back to the room, Nancy hit him again on exactly the same spot. He pulled the knife on her, and the play-acting which they had performed so often became real, as they both pushed forward at the same time.

Sid's initial confusion turned to despair, as he realized that he was alone, and he told reporters how distraught he was at losing Nancy. Nine days after a court hearing on 13 October allowed bail of $50,00 (put up by Virgin), Sid tried to commit suicide. He was taken to the psychiatric ward at Bellevue Hospital but discharged after a few days, and re-entered New York life with a new girl, Michelle Robinson.

Sid's bail was confirmed at a hearing on 21 November, although he was described, unimaginatively if accurately, as someone who 'cultivates an image of antagonism'. He proved the statement true less than three weeks later when he got into a fight

at a nightclub. He was arrested and taken to prison at Riker's Island, where it was decided he should remain in custody until his next court appearance scheduled for 1 February 1979.

A FOREGONE CONCLUSION

The enforced period without drugs meant that by then Sid was drug-free. McLaren planned to meet him the following day, when he was expected to be released, but the judge let him out on the day of the hearing. He went back to Michelle's flat along with his mother and a few friends where he succumbed and took some heroin.

After they had eaten a meal some more heroin was brought in. This supply was purer than usual, and the effect of this combined with Sid's detoxification caused him to collapse on the bed. He came round, however, and was left to sleep it off peacefully. However, some time during the night, he woke up, found the stash and took another hit. The next morning he was discovered to be dead.

Sid's 'textbook' rock death began his path to icon status, starting with the rumour that the urn containing his ashes had been dropped and smashed at Heathrow airport. The sleeve of a posthumously released EP, *Sid Sings*, showed a Sid Vicious Action Man lying in a coffin, an image that conveyed the double-edged truth in the myth of Sid Vicious – the toy soldier behind the street-fighter.

He was a malleable person, and could have been directed in many different ways, but once he had taken on his persona, there were few people around him who envisaged a happy ending for him.

▶ *On stage at the Winterland, San Francisco, where the Pistols gave their final show in front of 5,000 people and afterwards split up. Sid's reaction was to take an overdose before getting on a plane to New York.*

Index

The names of films, television programmes, books, plays, newspapers and record albums are in italics. The titles of singles are not.